THEY CALL ME
PUDGE

My Life Playing the Game I Love

*Ivan Rodriguez
with Jeff Sullivan*

TRIUMPH
BOOKS

Library of Congress Cataloging-in-Publication Data
    Names: Rodriguez, Ivan, author. | Sullivan, Jeff, author.
    Title: They call me Pudge : my life playing the game I love / Ivan
        Rodriguez with Jeff Sullivan.
    Description: Chicago, Illinois : Triumph Books, [2017]
    Identifiers: LCCN 2017011870 | ISBN 9781629373942
    Subjects: LCSH: Rodriguez, Ivan | Baseball players—Puerto
        Rico—Biography.
    Classification: LCC GV865.R623 R64 2017 | DDC 796.357092
        [B] —dc23 LC record available at https://lccn.loc.
        gov/2017011870

This book is available in quantity at special discounts for your group or organization. For further information, contact:
    Triumph Books LLC
    814 North Franklin Street
    Chicago, Illinois 60610
    (312) 337-0747
    www.triumphbooks.com

Printed in U.S.A.

ISBN: 978-1-62937-394-2

Design by Patricia Frey and Sue Knopf

To my parents, Jose and Eva,
for all their love, inspiration, and sacrifice

Contents

Foreword

I KNOW FROM FIRSTHAND EXPERIENCE HOW DIFFICULT BEING called up to the big leagues at 19 years old can be. And when the Texas Rangers brought Pudge up in 1991, he was actually a couple weeks younger than I was when the New York Mets promoted me in 1966. It's funny to think about really, but after I made my debut, Pudge wouldn't be born for another five years—yet I was fortunate enough to pitch to him for three seasons.

During his first game—at Comiskey Park in Chicago—he threw out a couple of guys on the bases, and I don't think they were even close. He was throwing some heat for sure. I remember hearing he was clocked at 94 miles per hour throwing down to second base. There were times he was throwing the ball back to the pitcher with more velocity than they were throwing it to him. I think we would both say our ability to throw a baseball was a God-given gift.

The next day, which would have been June 21, was the first time Pudge caught me. We made some history, too. It was one of the few times a teenager caught a pitcher more than 40 years old. In other words, a kid catching an old timer.

Back then Pudge didn't speak much, if any, English, and this won't surprise anyone, but I don't speak any Spanish. So when we met in the coaches' room of the clubhouse for our pregame scouting report, well, it wasn't a long discussion. I told him, "You put the fingers down, and I'll throw it. And we're going to have ourselves a good night."

Pudge just kept calling pitches until I shook my head yes. Then he'd go to location, and I would shake yes when we were at the right place. And we got along quite well. I allowed just one hit that first start. After the game I walked into manager Bobby Valentine's office and I said, "This kid is alright. I'd be just fine throwing to him from now on."

A few starts later in Arlington on July 7, I was cruising along through seven innings of what would have been my eighth no-hitter. We were playing the California Angels, and Dave Winfield singled up the middle on an 0–2 pitch to lead off the eighth. After the game, which we won 7–0, reporters asked Pudge about the pitch to Winfield, and he said I shook him off. So he did learn to speak English pretty quickly.

The following spring training—and this is one of Pudge's favorite stories—he says he hit a home run off me to center field. During his next time up, the ball somehow got away from me, and I hit him in the leg. I don't remember the home run, but I do remember hitting him.

Around that time I remember thinking that Pudge was going to be one of the great ones. One would be hard-pressed to argue that he isn't the best all-around catcher to ever play the game. He became a much better hitter than I think anyone envisioned early on, and his 13 Gold Glove awards speak volumes. Only the great Brooks Robinson has won more among position players.

When Robin Ventura charged the mound in 1993, which was during my last year pitching, Pudge was right there trying to hold him off. What folks might not know—or remember—is that he had undergone facial surgery for a fractured cheekbone 40 hours earlier. Pudge was wearing a big bandage, but there he was, trying to protect his pitcher. It was ridiculous he was even catching that night.

Everyone likes to talk about my no-hitters and strikeouts, and I'm very proud of those accomplishments. You know what, though? For almost any professional athlete, the No. 1 goal is being able to take the field, so that you can be there for your teammates. So in that regard, Pudge and I share a great feat. In the modern era, no pitcher has started more games than my 773. And no one has caught more games than Pudge's 2,427. I know we both take a lot of pride in that. Many highly touted rookies come into the league and have immediate success—only to disappear a few years later. It takes a certain kind of determination and focus to produce every day season after season. And you need to work harder as you grow older; trust me on that.

Now, we were both fortunate to avoid any major injuries, but at the same time, playing 20-plus years doesn't happen by accident—especially at such a physically demanding position as catcher. A lot of younger guys aren't really into working out, and they don't have to be at that age. Not Pudge, though. He was putting himself through workouts almost every day from his rookie season. I was always really impressed by that. He wanted to be the best he could and not just rely on his natural talent.

It was a pleasure to have called Pudge a teammate. He represented what's good about baseball. He enjoyed playing the game. He truly loved every moment he was out there. From when he was that 19-year-old rookie in Chicago to his final game two decades later, he went out and played hard every day. He was that rare player who really left it all on the field. I know his fans appreciated that and I know his teammates and coaches did as well.

I am honored that we are not only linked as batterymates, but also as members of the Baseball Hall of Fame. More importantly, though, I'm honored to call him my friend—though I still don't recall him hitting that home run off me.

—Nolan Ryan
Texas Rangers pitcher 1989–1993

Foreword

OVER HIS FIRST 15 YEARS IN THE BIG LEAGUES, I DIDN'T SEE MUCH of Pudge Rodriguez. Our paths only crossed at All-Star Games and an interleague series during his MVP season in 1999. Obviously, though, I was well aware he was a superstar. I think we all knew that. Pudge was one of the faces of baseball for a long time—first with the Texas Rangers and then winning a World Series with the Florida Marlins. He was one of those guys your eyes gravitated toward when watching a game because of his intensity, his brilliant talent, and his childlike love of the game.

When Pudge signed with Detroit in 2004, that was the first big move in the team turning around its fortunes. This was a team coming off 119 losses the season before, and here was one of the game's elite players saying, Yeah, I'm committed to this franchise, and we're going to start winning. For general manager Dave Dombrowski, that signing was huge in terms of changing the atmosphere. That's where it all started. Other players were added later like Magglio Ordonez and Kenny Rogers, and some younger guys came up like Justin Verlander and Curtis Granderson, but all of that began with signing Pudge.

I came on board as manager in 2006, and we had a heck of a team there. We were ready to win and win we did. We went 95–67 and won the American League pennant before losing in five games to the St. Louis Cardinals in the World Series.

One of the first conversations I had at spring training that season was with Pudge. I let him know that we needed him to be a leader, that I wanted him to be vocal. You have to be careful with that as a manager, too. You don't want to put too much pressure on a guy in that situation to the point that the responsibility takes away from his focus on playing. Pudge handled it perfectly. It also helped because when you have a player of that magnitude—he was already one of the greatest catchers to ever play the game at that point—he commanded instant respect. This was the face of our team; this was a player with the highest status an active guy can have. That went a long way—both on the field and in the clubhouse.

Pudge was more or less what I expected as a ballplayer. He brought such a passion for the game, and his ability was off the charts. Even at 34 years old, his arm was just at another level from every other catcher. He led the league that season, throwing out 51 percent of base stealers. The league average was 30 percent.

The greatest example he set was this: no one worked harder than Pudge, and there was no question about it. No one who ever played for me outworked this guy. He'd be working out on the road at 8:00 in the morning. No one does that after a night game, especially after catching nine innings. He was smart enough to know that—in order to maintain the level of play he expected—he needed to outwork everyone. Only the great ones understand that. Not the very good players who come into the league with all this talent and have a nice eight or 10-year career. The great ones pride themselves in sustaining their excellence in the longevity of their careers.

I coached Carlton Fisk with the Chicago White Sox, and he would work out after games, too. No one else was working out, but he wanted to keep playing and having success. The two Pudges were alike in that regard. They were fanatics in terms of staying in shape, especially later in their careers.

Everyone talks about Pudge's arm, how well he moved side-to-side behind the plate, and his hitting, but he was also excellent at calling a game. He really did a superb job making in-game adjustments, too. A gameplan can become disruptive pretty quickly if a guy's best pitch isn't working, or maybe his second or third pitch is really working on a given night, and Pudge made those changes seamlessly even during a given inning.

Pudge had so many big hits for us and threw so many guys out, but you know what stands out for me looking back? His energy. He came to the park with a bunch of energy every day and he was such a competitor, one of those guys who wanted to succeed in every at-bat. He was so much fun to watch play the game he loves so much. Pudge set the tone for our teams. He had this enthusiasm like a kid. He enjoyed playing in the big leagues like a Little Leaguer—with the piss and vinegar rubbing off on all of us.

For the longest time, I said Johnny Bench was the greatest catcher I had ever seen myself. I played against him in the minor leagues way back when and I couldn't believe what I was seeing. Then I watched him on the Big Red Machine, those Cincinnati Reds teams he played for.

I'll tell you what, though, you can certainly make the case for Pudge, too. There's a reason that Pudge and Bench are the only two first-ballot catchers ever elected to the Hall of Fame. That's your starting point right there.

There's nothing I wouldn't do for Pudge. Coming to the ballpark every day and watching him play for us with the Tigers, that was a real joy for me. I was incredibly fortunate to manage him and I very much cherish the time we spent together.

—Jim Leyland
Detroit Tigers manager 2006–2013

THEY CALL ME
PUDGE

1

*Hall of Fame
and Clearing the Air*

THE DAYS BEFORE THE HALL OF FAME RESULTS WERE ANNOUNCED on January 18, 2017, I was a mess. I'm pretty sure that's the most nervous I have ever been in my life. I was barely sleeping. I've never been much of a drinker, but I had a few those nights. I knew the vote was going to be close—someone told me the night before that mine could very well be the closest vote ever. This was my first time on the ballot. Some didn't see the big deal of being selected the first time around, but for me it was incredibly important.

There was a lot of praying those days before the announcement. My wife, Patricia, stayed with me almost every moment. As always, she was my spiritual guide when I needed her most. We stayed up late, which I have always been guilty of, even as a kid. The only difference was that I wasn't really going to sleep when the sun came up. The more stressed I became, Patricia would pray more and more.

First, since I was seven years old, my goal has been to enter the Hall of Fame. There were obviously other goals—daily, seasonal, long-term—but first and foremost, nothing drove me more than wanting to be a Hall of Famer. To me that's the ultimate. That's everything; that's how we as athletes, as baseball players, are validated.

Also, my favorite player, my hero really, growing up was Johnny Bench. I wanted to do everything like him. And he was the only catcher to ever be elected on the first ballot. Well, just because I'm not a kid anymore doesn't mean I stopped wanting to do everything like Johnny Bench. I wanted to join him in being elected the first time around. I wanted to have that honor. I wanted to stand on that stage in Cooperstown with him as equals.

In fact, nothing made me happier in the days leading up to the vote when I saw some comments from Bench in *The Dallas Morning News*, saying: "He should be a lock. As complete a catcher as I've ever seen. He was intimidating behind the plate, a real solid hitter and incredibly durable. He is everything you'd hope for at the position."

Told that I had caught 20,000 innings, more than any other catcher and 650 more games than him, Bench said, "Those are crazy numbers. I had 17 broken bones in my body. I got to a point where I simply couldn't physically do it anymore. He kept doing it—and at a high level—for much longer. For him to endure the beating he took back there and keep playing, those numbers alone show that he belongs."

Look, I'm a competitive person. And as the day approached, I became more and more competitive, driven—I guess even obsessed—about the vote. I had zero interest in waiting another year. That's a long time waiting and thinking about why I wasn't elected my first year of eligibility. That year would have been torture.

And I'd like to think my numbers speak for themselves. The 13 Gold Gloves, which is a record for catchers, the 2,427 games caught, which is 201 more than Hall of Famer Carlton Fisk, who ranks second. I was known for my defense, which was always my primary focus, but I could hit a little, too. I had 2,844 hits, 311 home runs, almost a .300 career batting average. And I even stole 127 bases—not bad for a guy called Pudge.

I also won the American League MVP award in 1999 and seven Silver Sluggers as the league's best hitting catcher. Then there was the National League Championship Series MVP in 2003, when my Florida Marlins won the World Series.

Honestly, there was no reason the vote should even be close.

Well, it was. You need 75 percent of the vote, which this year meant 332 votes. I received 336 or 76 percent. The great Jackie Robinson received 77.5 during his first year of eligibility.

When the call came a few moments before the official announcement on Major League Baseball Network, I had been furiously pacing at my friend's house in Dallas. I had flown in from Miami the day before because if I was voted in we wanted to hold the press conference at Globe Life Park in Arlington. Yes, I played for six teams, but in terms of baseball, the Rangers were and are my home. From the time they signed me as a 16-year-old in Puerto Rico who didn't speak English, that's where I grew up.

After I found out about my induction into the Hall of Fame, my reaction was captured for eternity, as I lifted my left arm and pumped my fist. It's pretty easy to find with a Google search. The smile on my face says it all. Almost immediately, the joy overwhelmed me, and I started crying. My son, Dereck, came over and hugged me. That only increased the tears. Then Patricia wrapped hr arms around me and told me how proud she was, how much she loved me, and how our prayers and faith led to this moment. To have a dream you have thought about every day for 37 years become a reality, there really aren't any words to capture what that feels like. The closest description is to say I was euphoric, overjoyed with so much happiness that you can barely feel your feet on the ground.

The next few hours were beautiful and chaotic. I never really understood that American expression that your "head is spinning." Well, I do now. My head was spinning, and my phone was blowing up. After a few minutes of celebrating with my family, we were off for the 30-minute ride to the press conference at the ballpark. Once there, I spoke from the heart, saying, "To be honest with you, I haven't slept in three days. I'm not kidding. A lot of good friends telling me you're going to be in, you're going to make it. But at the same time, I was receiving a lot of caution— like if it's not this year, it's next.

"I didn't want to hear that.

"What can I say? Growing up as a child in my hometown of Vega Baja, Puerto Rico, to go into the Hall of Fame…It's a great honor. I feel most proud to be in the Hall of Fame as a first-timer. It's not the second time or the fourth time. To be there in one of one is an honor."

The next morning, after finally grabbing a few hours of peaceful sleep, we were off to New York City. I was so proud. I joined my fellow inductees, Jeff Bagwell and Tim Raines, for a press conference. The official 2017 induction class also included former commissioner Bud Selig and longtime front-office executive John Schuerholz, who led the Kansas City Royals and Atlanta Braves to World Series championships, but they were selected a month earlier via the Veterans' Committee.

So, I threw out 661 base runners in my career, 46 percent of those who dared to run on me. Thing is, I never nailed Raines or Bagwell, who were a combined 5-for-5 off me. Raines was one of the best ever on the base paths, so that's understandable. And Bagwell just stole one time, so that gave us something to joke about before the press conference. Obviously, it's a great group of guys to be inducted with, and I've always had the utmost respect for Raines and Bagwell. We'll always be linked, so having that eternal connection is pretty cool as well.

The Hall of Fame is the biggest of deals. I am humbled to be included. Fewer than 1 percent of those who play Major League Baseball are elected, and that's not even factoring in all those whose dreams died in the minor leagues. And of that 1 percent fortunate enough to be elected to Cooperstown, about 16 percent have been on the first ballot. And at 45 years old, I'm (for the moment) the youngest member of the Hall of Fame. Also, I'm quite proud to be the fourth Puerto Rican, joining Roberto Clemente, Orlando Cepeda, and Roberto Alomar. No other Latino country has produced more than two since World War II.

Those were the happiest few days of my life with the exception of my three children being born. For me, some of the questions that were being asked, it didn't matter. I'm a Hall of Famer, and the Rangers were retiring my No. 7 as well. That's all that matters. I couldn't be happier.

As for those questions, I'm happy to address them. I've never avoided them. There's so much misinformation and witch hunting when it comes to that era. Just because Jose Canseco writes something in a book, that doesn't make it fact. I don't hold grudges, so I've seen Jose since then and I shook his hand. That's what men do. I'm sure he had his reasons. Thing is, from what I've been told since I've never read the book, Jose basically threw everyone and everything he could find under the bus. He was throwing so many guys under buses that he needed to bring in one of those double-deckers from London. When someone says everyone is guilty, and a few guys end up being guilty, that doesn't make them right.

I never took steroids. Let's make that as crystal clear as possible—I never took steroids. If anyone says differently, they are lying. Here's what I did do. I worked my ass off. I was a guy who played the game the right way. I was disciplined with my workouts and my diet. I worked as hard as I could to do the best I could—every day for 20-plus years. I loved the game of baseball. That was my life. My earliest memories involve baseball. I was blessed with an arm from God, one capable of throwing like few players ever have. And I focused on baseball every day. I would be up watching games or highlights until three or four in the morning after our night games.

As for my training, weight loss, and weight gains along the way, I was always kind of stocky. As a sophomore in high school, shortly before the Rangers signed me in July 1988, I was 5'7", 165 pounds with a whole bunch of baby fat still on me. At minor league camp in 1989, I had grown another inch, maybe two (the last time that would happen) and put on a few more pounds. It was there, in Port Charlotte, Florida, that an instructor, Chino Cadahia, first called me "Pudge." Obviously, it caught on. I was always okay with it. It's a fun nickname; I get it. If someone asks me nowadays what I prefer, I usually just say either Ivan or Pudge.

I was eating a little better in the minor leagues, though certainly not watching my diet. That's a lot easier to do at 17 and 18 years young. Looking back, I ate a ton of protein, lots of chicken fingers. And I just played a lot of baseball, so the baby fat started to fall off. Those first few years in the big leagues with the Rangers, I gained more weight, more muscle than fat, and during the 1994–95 offseason I met Edgar Diaz. I had just turned 23 years old.

He was also from Puerto Rico, an Olympic pole vaulter who was a few years older than I was. I was playing winter ball and I guess he came to my game that day. Later that night he walked up to me at a restaurant called Lupi's, which is owned by former big league pitcher Ed Figueroa, and said, "By any chance, does your right knee hurt?"

Well, yes, my knee was bothering me some, and I wondered how in the world he knew that. I wasn't limping. My father taught me pretty early on not to show any weakness. Edgar explained that I was running incorrectly, that my toes, butt, and knees weren't lifting. I asked him if he could fix it, and he said yes and that I should meet him at the track the next day at 4:00 PM. I was there 10 minutes early, and we ran a bunch of different drills together. That became a daily ritual. I asked him to join me in Texas, so we could train during the season, and we've been together since. Even to this day, if I want to work out, I usually give him a call.

I was around 230 pounds the winter I met Edgar. His plan was to train me like a sprinter. He wanted me to lose weight, and within 18 months, I was down to 198. The new training schedule certainly wasn't easy, but there were immediate signs of progress. I had better strength, quickness, and explosiveness, especially later in games. My arm and swing were faster, too.

My power numbers improved, which is completely natural for any younger player. Offensively, the average big leaguer peaks at about 27 years old, which was how old I was for my MVP season of 1999. That year I hit 35 home runs. I probably would have hit 30 the two following years as well if not for injuries. I was never a power hitter, though. During my 16-year peak run from 1992 to 2007, I averaged 30 doubles and 18 home runs per season.

At the conclusion of the 1998 campaign, I told Edgar that I wanted to win the American League MVP award the following year. My teammate, Juan Gonzalez, who incidentally was from the same town in Puerto Rico as me, had won the honor two of the previous three seasons, and I always wanted to push myself.

What better way to push myself more than being considered the best player in the game, right?

EDGAR DIAZ
PERSONAL TRAINER

"I told him, 'Hey, if you want to be an MVP, let's go train harder.' I also suggested that he not play winter ball in Puerto Rico that offseason, just dedicate himself to training and rest. After they lost to the Yankees in the first round of the playoffs in 1998, I told him to rest. 'Just enjoy life, do whatever you need to do, vacation, whatnot. And on November 1, we're going to take measurements and start training like never before.' That's what we did, and the baseball world saw the results the next year. We trained at least three hours every day that winter, three weeks on, one week off. In the afternoons he would work on his swing or other parts of his game, just not play in actual games, which was tough on him. He loves playing baseball so much.

"If you want to play for seven months during the season, you cannot train for just six weeks during the offseason. There's no way anyone can do that without getting muscle tears and wearing down. We ran 300 and 400-meter reps, did some weights, more reps and less weight, a lot of core stuff. He really started eating properly.

"During the 1999 season, I saw all 162 games. Sometimes he would wake me up at 3:00 in the morning and say he was having back pain or something. And I would go over there and give him treatment. I was a trainer, a physical therapist, a psychologist, everything. From that moment until now, we've been like brothers.

"Once he got his weight to 198 he stayed there for two or three years. But I had to tell him not to get too skinny because of his position and the amount of energy it required. Since catchers are always moving up and down so much, they have to store their energy in a little bit of fat. Pudge never went down below 8 percent body fat. He stayed at that level.

"I can't tell you how many times we would finish a workout, and Ivan would say, 'That's it? We're finished for today? I feel like I can do more.' He's a workaholic. He loves the game so much and he had that rare drive to strive to be the best."

My diet also changed as my career progressed, as I think happens with just about any professional athlete. And really, if you want to avoid being overweight, it probably applies to most people. When I was younger, I could eat whatever I wanted and, with all the calories I was burning off playing baseball, I was still skinny. I ate everything, though honestly, I was never a big candy or soda guy. After I met Edgar, though, especially in the offseason when we were training, there was a huge focus on protein like red meat, white meat, turkey, chicken, fish, or beef. All the proteins affect your body differently, so you can't just eat the same kind all the time.

Edgar and I worked out during the season, too, though those were much lighter obviously. We'd warm up; stretch; maybe run an 800-meter on the track; work on knee kicks, lunges, and more stretching. We focused on speed resistance and making sure I had the same energy every day. Even if we went extra innings, I wanted to feel the same as I did in the first inning.

I've always been hyper, so that meant usually going to sleep late. The good part of that is: once I fell asleep, I slept hard. We focused a lot on hydration and getting a lot of nutrients. And if I was eating healthy, there was no need for other kinds of stuff like supplements. I did take a lot of protein shakes or amino acids. In addition to eating well, resting, drinking lots of water, that's all you need. If you train well, work hard, and make the sacrifices needed, then you don't need anything extra.

Two other points I want to clarify: yes, I lost 25 pounds during the 2004–05 offseason. This caused some speculation since it was after Canseco's book came out, and the league was finally starting to become serious about testing. The truth is my first wife, Maribel, and I were going through a divorce at that time, and it was horrible. I don't think anyone besides those closest to me could know how tough that was, how much it drained me physically and mentally. It was a low point.

There was no training that offseason, at least in the sense of how Edgar and I had been doing it. Looking back, I was probably depressed. I wasn't eating well, not so much bad food, just not eating much, not getting the protein I needed. I was sleeping worse than usual. My only outlet was going for bike rides. I started going for long rides, whether it be the stationary bike or outside. I would ride 20 or 30 miles a day. That was most of the offseason.

And I felt better once I arrived at camp. I was 33 years old and had been catching in the big leagues for 15 years. I had a hip flexor injury the year before that really hindered me behind the plate. What works at 27 doesn't at 33 or 38. So during that season and going forward, I did a lot more running, sprints, stretching, and fewer weights.

Secondly, if you look at my career, my body kind of performed as it was supposed to. I was mostly healthy in my 20s and sustained more and more injuries later in my career. Heck, I didn't even hit 20 home runs in a single season after turning 30. My career followed the path it should have, and I worked damn hard in the offseason to stay in the condition I needed to. Fisk and Bob Boone, who rank second and third behind me in games caught, were able to catch well into their 40s. I wasn't. I was 39 years old during my last season. I only have the record of games caught because I was fortunate enough to start my big league career at 19.

I really don't know what else to say on the subject except this: I don't begrudge any player from that era who did take whatever they did. It was a tough time with different rules, and no one really knew what was going on. It happened, and everyone seems to have moved forward, which is best for the game. I hope the great players from that time who are deserving are one day able to join me in the Hall of Fame.

2

More Than a Pastime

I WAS BORN ON NOVEMBER 27, 1971, THOUGH MY BIRTHDAY IS often reported as being three days thereafter, to my parents, Jose and Eva. My brother Tito, who is two years older than me, rounded out our family.

We lived in Vega Baja, a small, country town in Puerto Rico. We never had much money, but we never really thought of it that way. We were kind of like everyone else in our town so we never thought about how other people were living. I had a bike, a skateboard, and our family had a television. There was always food on the table, too. That's really all a kid needs, right?

I started playing baseball when I was seven years old, but I also played different sports. I was a really good volleyball player—but not so much basketball because of my height. When I scored my first basket, everyone celebrated like we won the championship. That likely was also my last basket.

I grew up in a family that played sports. My dad was a baseball player, a slugging left fielder, and my mom played in a few softball leagues with him when we were growing up. My uncles and cousins all played, and I started falling in love with baseball because it gave me a chance to be around the family. Even though I played other sports, my dad was the one to tell me he would love to see me play the game of baseball. For my father baseball in many ways was an extension of life, as vital as oxygen. He would tell me, "Outside of family, baseball has been everything for me, my happiness, my satisfaction with the world."

My dad was my first coach. He was my teacher in the beginning. And then I started playing in leagues in Puerto Rico. I was a natural. I always had a good arm and threw the ball hard. One of the first positions I played was pitcher. I threw seven no-hitters, including two in one day. And I hit a lot of kids because the ball went everywhere. If it was a strike, it was a pretty good pitch, but if it wasn't a strike, I didn't know where it was going. They always kept me in the game even when I wasn't pitching because I was very good with my glove, could play a mean third base, and hit well.

When I was seven, I was a normal-sized kid, but after that everyone else started to pass me. By the age of 12 or 13, I was very short. I just didn't grow as fast as the other kids. I even started doing some exercises to try to stretch my body and grow taller. One day I left school early, and nobody was at the house. I decided to hang by my arms from a rope, dangling off our second-floor balcony so that I could grow. I had a step to get up there, but I slipped and stayed there hanging from the rope, almost getting choked until my dad came in. And I'm lucky he came home when he did. It was scary, I mean can you imagine everyone thinking I hung myself when I was such a happy kid? It's funny now, but it wasn't at the time. I guess it shows how insecure I was about being short.

My brother and I had two parents that everybody would be lucky to have. Mom and Dad wanted to make sure that everything was okay for us. They were very serious, strict parents, and we lived with rules. We had a set amount of time to play, to do our homework, to eat dinner, and to get ready for bed. And if we weren't in bed at the right time, they were going to be mad.

Our family time was at dinner. One of my parents' biggest rules was that we were going to eat together. That wasn't up for debate. At 6:30 or so, the four of us would be sitting at the table. We would usually talk about our day or, as we grew older, baseball.

Everything in our house revolved around baseball. My brother and I used to play in our room with a rolled-up piece of paper and shower shoes. The paper was the ball, the shoes were the bats, and we used a book as the strike zone. We would sit on the floor and play every night, sometimes for hours before going to bed. It was an open house with wood paneling, so our parents could hear everything going on in our room. We would play so late and end up so tired that some mornings my mother would have to drop water on our faces to wake us up.

EVA RODRIGUEZ
MOTHER

"They actually started playing that game in the bedroom with socks and their hands. Ivan was a pretty calm boy. He liked being around his mother. He was well-mannered and somewhat shy. But wow, was he active—riding bikes, racing Hot Wheels all over the house, playing hide-and-seek. When he was 10, he was trying out new ways to ride his bike, and one of those ways was with no hands. He's showing off to his friends, lost control, and drove into a barbwire fence. There was a lot of bleeding that day.

"He liked to swim and watch cartoons and baseball games on the TV, but he was always happiest playing baseball. Even at that younger age, Ivan always had this charisma that you can't teach. I think he was born with it."

Both of my parents worked incredibly hard. My mom started her own hair styling business and then went back to school to become a teacher after my brother and I were born. She taught second grade for more than 20 years, took some time off, and then worked as a school director for another 14 years. My father worked as an electrician, spending his whole career with a company called Daniel Construction. They produced electricity for different pharmacies around the island of Puerto Rico. He was a foreman and had a big group of employees working for him.

However, it wasn't easy. They worked hard to make sure we had food at the house, had good clothes and shoes to wear to school, and every single thing that we needed. I remember that we used to have the best baseball gear—good batting gloves, good spikes, great bats—compared to the other kids. Pretty much my whole Little League team used my bat because my dad bought us the best stuff. I would use the bat for a couple years until new equipment came out. That's when he would go to the sporting goods store, buy it, and come home to give it to us. Those were the magical days of my childhood. Yeah, throwing a no-hitter or hitting a home run was big, but new equipment, that was the mountaintop.

I wasn't a very good student, to be honest with you. It was hard for me because I couldn't concentrate while sitting in the classroom and listening to the teacher for over an hour. Maybe I had attention-deficit disorder, but no one knew what that was back then. My brother, on the other hand, was a good student. I think my father and I are the same; we just didn't have that passion for school. But my parents made me work hard. My mother would sit at the dinner table and work with me on homework every night. Then she would make me study after I finished my homework. Do the homework, then study that homework for another 40 minutes. Read back and forth, back and forth, back and forth. And I got better because of her help. But I still didn't learn much because I had my mind on playing baseball from a very early age. I would sit in that classroom running through baseball scenarios in my head or I would be reviewing the game from the day before, thinking, *What could I have done differently, how could I be better?*

While I wasn't an A-student in the classroom, I was an A-plus student on the baseball field. I was a quick learner and picked up everything they taught me. And I put it into action. Over the years my parents found out, *Hey, there is something very special in this kid.* School was still a priority, but now they were thinking more seriously about baseball. Sometimes they would even pull me out of class early to take me to baseball practice. They knew something special was going on with me.

I never wanted to be anything else but a baseball player. I guess if there was no baseball I would have loved to be a truck driver. I love trucks. Every time I'm on the freeway, I love to see the big 18-wheelers. It's been that way since I was little. My parents would always buy me gasoline-semi or container-semi toy trucks. That was something I always thought about. But in my mind, I knew that's not what I really wanted to be. I wanted to be a baseball player.

As a young pitcher, at times, I was unhittable. I always hit for power and I was always on base, but the highlights of my Little League career were as a pitcher. Every time I pitched, I pitched the whole game, five innings at first and seven innings later on. If I was throwing a no-hitter, I would be unaware because we never had scoreboards. I didn't know until after the last out when my coach would tell me. All the parents would be excited and jumping and having fun, watching me pitch and strike everybody out.

I hit a lot of kids with my fastball—even some good friends of mine. And some of them never played again because they were scared after I hit them. Obviously, that made me feel bad, seeing a kid on the ground crying after I hit him. But what I really didn't like was the tension it caused between my parents and the other kids' parents. Sometimes I could see them yelling at each other when I looked into the bleachers. I didn't want anybody to say anything bad about my mom or dad because I would get very upset. It wasn't their fault. I wasn't trying to hit the other kid. It just would happen because the pitch ran away.

Eventually, my father decided that my pitching days were behind me. That wasn't my call. In fact, I immediately started crying and didn't stop for 20 minutes. I didn't want to catch. I wanted to throw no-hitters and hit home runs playing third base. In all fairness to my father, it wasn't only him. One of my coaches, the legendary Julio Pabon, once said in an interview, "We had to stop him from pitching because the velocity he had was too much. He honestly could have killed one of the kids with the stuff he was throwing."

Jose Rodriguez
Father

"On his senior youth team, which would have been when he was nine years old, Ivan set the league record for strikeouts and no-hitters by a pitcher. Soon after at a regional tournament called La Ilanura, he hit three batters to load the bases, and I took him out. I told him then and there he was going to be a catcher and, if he didn't like changing positions, I would never come see him play or coach him ever again. I'm glad he listened to his father. I've coached so many players over the years and I've never seen one so disciplined and dedicated as Ivan. For the longest time, he would wear his uniform to bed on Friday night for Saturday morning games.

"Once he was catching, Ivan learned very fast. If you showed him a specific technique, he could replicate it immediately. He was a catching savant in many ways. And he never wanted to stop. He'd come home from a doubleheader, have a quick meal, and ask me or his brother to come outside to work on drills. We'd throw hundreds of balls in the dirt so he could block them. He'd never tire; he just wanted to play more baseball. I have never witnessed a work ethic in my life like my son's. Yes, God gave him much talent, but he also maximized that talent like few in this world do. Ivan was already one of the better catchers on the island at 13 years old."

And that's how I started catching. In Puerto Rico we used to play doubleheaders on Saturdays, so I would either pitch in the morning and catch in the afternoon or catch in the morning and pitch in the afternoon. It made for some very long days, but when you're one of the best players on the team, you're going to see more action. Yes, when we had no pitchers left, they still let me pitch on occasion. I still enjoyed pitching a lot. I don't know whether I had the stuff to make it to the big leagues, though I doubt it because of my height. Back then teams loved to sign big, tall pitchers who were six feet or taller. One year the Philadelphia Phillies' pitching staff was made up of players all 6'4" and up. That's why my dad told me, "I'd like to see you catch because you have the frame, you're strong, and you certainly have the arm." I stopped pitching for good when I was 13 or 14.

I ended up 5'9". My dad is about 5'8", and my mom is 5'4", (and that might be generous). So I knew I wasn't going to be tall. But what's strange is, even though both my parents are very short and me and my ex-wife, the mother of my kids, are both short, I have a son who is 6'3". My dad's father was over six feet tall, and on my mother's side, my grandpa was 6'5". My dad's brothers are six feet or taller, but my brother and I are the same height. Just one of those things, I guess. Maybe I would have been a Cy Young award winner if I was 6'3", but, of course, I wouldn't change a thing. The catching thing worked out okay, right?

As a coach my father pushed me but in a good way. The way he did it was in a well-meaning way. He knew that when you have a good player you have to take everything that kid has and help him grow. That's an important thing. Usually, the fathers you see who are yelling and screaming at their kids in Little League games, well, their kids don't have the talent to be that good. They just aren't ballplayers.

My dad pushed me, but he wasn't a guy who would scream at me. He was always there, though, watching me from behind the fence when I was catching. When I looked back, he was right there. He also went all over the field, calling balls and strikes, even though he wasn't a catcher. My uncles and my father were very good baseball players at the time. They didn't play professionally, but they played in the local leagues. My father was a power hitter and he could hit balls way out of the ballpark.

I had to learn a lot about catching later on in my development because in Little League the runners stayed on the bag. They would only attempt to steal when the ball got past the hitter. But I definitely learned from my dad how to call the game. He told me to move inside, move outside, don't stay in the middle of the plate, keep my glove down, and remember what the hitters had done in their last at-bat. I learned that at a very early age because he told me all about it. Those lessons, that advice, I was still using that in the big leagues. The fundamentals never change either. And you can never master them enough. A young catcher shouldn't worry about snap throws to first base until they know how to block a ball to either side of them and throw down to second.

When we went home, it wasn't just to watch a soap opera or something. We talked baseball. Baseball, baseball, and more baseball. That even includes my mother, who would come to the games and get fired up enough to scream at the umpires. We talked about what I did in the game, why I made this decision or that one. We talked about everything, and it was an enjoyable conversation. We would talk about it for 30 or 40 minutes, and then it was over with. They would let us be kids after that, and we could go play in the yard or do whatever else we wanted—unless, that is, there was a baseball game on television that night.

The *Game of the Week* was mandatory in my parents' eyes, and we didn't do anything else when it was on. We were all on the sofa by 7:00 PM and watched the entire game with nothing in our hands, nothing to distract us from what was happening on the field. In Puerto Rico at that time, they used to air a lot of Cincinnati Reds games because of Tony Perez, so I saw a lot of Johnny Bench, who, as I mentioned earlier, was my favorite player. He did everything correctly. My father would tell me to watch him behind the plate, and I couldn't take my eyes off him. And he wasn't huge, either—just 6'1", not even 200 pounds—so that kind of made me think that I could catch in the big leagues. Bench, though, was actually my favorite player even before I started catching. He put up some huge numbers, hit more than 40 home runs twice, won two National League MVP awards, and earned 10 straight Gold Gloves, a record until someone else came along.

They also aired a lot of Detroit Tigers games, and I loved the bright orange and black catcher's mitt that Lance Parrish wore. I told my dad, "I would love to have that kind of glove one day," and he went out and bought one for me. More than anyone, though, I always enjoyed watching Bench and what he did. He was an exceptional, aggressive catcher who threw the ball everywhere. He was also a good hitter who played the game hard. A lot of what I was doing as a young catcher growing up came from what I saw him do.

As a young player, I was always focused, anticipating, thinking about what would happen next. I was a shy kid who didn't talk much, but when it came to the game of baseball, I was another person. My dad taught me how to respect the game, especially if he saw me losing my temper. I did throw bats. I did throw helmets. And I got punished. He would sit me down and not let me play in the game. That was my punishment. I would have preferred getting hit with a belt to that. After I threw a bat or threw a helmet, my dad would make me go pick it up. And if I threw a helmet in the dirt, he would make me pick it up, clean it, and put it back in the right place. He would tell me, "Don't do that because discipline is very important. I want you to be a good, disciplined player. I want you to set an example."

He was trying to teach me what to do instead of getting upset, and what he was saying was true. My temper got a lot better by the time I reached the big leagues, but it was still there. I, though, might have let it show in the runway behind the dugout instead of on the field. It was because I cared so much, and sometimes that's not a bad thing. As a player I would love to hear another big leaguer, throwing shit around because I knew that guy cared. That's the way I looked at it. It has to come from the heart. If I had four at-bats, I wanted to have five hits. If I was catching, I wanted to catch a no-hitter every day and I wanted to throw every single runner out because I was pushing myself to be great. I had the ability to be good, but I wanted to be better.

One of the keys for me, and this is a good lesson for young kids, especially beginners, is to make them put the catching gear on first. And let them know that the catching gear will be all the protection they need to have for the position. The mask is going to protect your face, so don't be afraid of the baseball. That's something my father taught me—you're not going to get hurt. Don't turn your head away from the ball. When you do, the side of your head is unprotected. That's the way he taught me, and that's the way I will teach every single young kid. If I ask them if they want to catch, they better give me an honest answer. Because that's not an easy position to play. You need to be ready to be a catcher, and there are not too many people who can do it. I enjoyed catching as a kid because it kept me in the game and kept me focused. Behind the plate you're calling the pitches, you're catching, you're receiving the ball, and you're throwing it back. I loved to be in the game and I was a part of every pitch when my team was on the field. Standing in the outfield for several innings without having to make a play, that would have been really tough on me.

There's a difference between throwing the ball as a pitcher and as a catcher. When you pitch, you're able to wind up, bring your leg back, and have all the force carrying you forward. As a catcher you're just able to move your feet. A pitcher can release the ball from anywhere, but as a catcher, you always have to throw it from the ear because that helps you stay low. It's two different types of throws. Outfielders throw different from infielders, the infielders throw different from the catcher, and the pitcher has the advantage of using different angles to throw the ball.

When I was in the prime of my career, I could throw the ball 92 or 93 miles per hour all the way from home plate to second base. But if I tried throwing off the rubber to home plate, I might only throw 88. That's the truth. For example, I cannot throw the ball like Gold Glove third baseman Adrian Beltre from third to first, and Beltre cannot throw the ball from home to second base the way I do. It's just different.

I think, like almost anywhere, some of the fields in Puerto Rico were good, some were bad, and some were horrible. Some had big pieces of rock in the infield. In the park where we grew up, there was a huge piece of rock along the first-base line, stretching almost all the way to first base. We just had to run around it. I didn't care, though, because I just wanted to wear my uniform and play baseball. On Saturdays when we had morning games, I would wake up early, already in my uniform after having slept in it, and head to the backyard. I would jog back and forth to warm up. Then I would have my father or brother play catch with me. We'd have a quick breakfast and then be off to the field. It's really hard to describe how excited I was those mornings we had a game. I could barely have a discussion of any kind if it wasn't about the game.

One memory that has stayed with me is when they would hand out uniforms the day before the season started. I'd race home and change into it. I wouldn't take it off for a few days. There were many nights I slept with my catcher's mitt, too.

A big step in my development came at 13 when my father moved me to San Juan so I could train at the Raiders Baseball Academy, which was one of the best in the country and run by Luis Rosa. There were scouts there every day. We traveled as a team all over the place—both in Puerto Rico and the United States. The first time we flew to Florida for a weekend tournament was actually my first time leaving Puerto Rico. We won just about all of our tournaments and we were a loaded team.

The first scout to talk to my father was Manny Batista, who was with the Texas Rangers, and he's the one who made it possible for me to join the academy. I played there a couple of years, and then at 16, that was when some of my teammates started to sign big league contracts. There was a prospect showcase in San Juan with a bunch of teams in attendance. Sandy Johnson and Omar Minaya were there for the Rangers, along with Manny.

Rosa had four catchers lined up that day to run, throw, hit— all that good stuff they have you do at showcases and tryouts. I was the last one of the bunch, which I wasn't happy about. Rosa thought the other catchers were better prospects, I guess. Actually, going into that showcase, we knew there was interest from the Kansas City Royals and San Diego Padres, but they both wanted me to play second base because of my height. I was 5'7" at the time. That's when my dad stepped up and said, "If you think you're going to sign my kid as a second baseman, you're wasting your time. He's a catcher."

That was the end of those discussions. That left the Rangers as the only team interested in me as a catcher.

SANDY JOHNSON
RANGERS SCOUTING DIRECTOR
"I'm in the dugout and this scout, Doug Gassaway, comes running in from the outfield, saying that this little guy just threw 93 miles an hour to second base. He's talking about Pudge. Why he was out there clocking catchers throwing to second base, I have no idea, but he was. I told Luis Rosa we liked him. Luis had these four other catchers he liked, and they all signed and got big money, but I told him we didn't

care about those guys. We wanted Pudge. He was only 150, 160 pounds at the most, but he had a loose, live arm, great hands, and he could swing the bat. I'd like to say how smart I was to find a Hall of Famer, but we backed into that one. Pudge wasn't Pudge [at 16 years old].

"He was all business from Day One. There was no playing around. He had pride in what he was doing. He wanted to be good. He was determined to be good. If he had a bad day, he was almost distraught because he was determined to be the best."

In literally 10 minutes, I went from the last catcher on the tryout list to the first, so I put the gear on and headed out to the plate. They threw me a few pitches to watch my receiving skills. They saw I had soft hands and after the fourth throw they stopped me and said, "We don't need to see anymore."

Next up was throwing to second base. After I made my first throw, they said, "You don't need to throw anymore." One throw. They didn't care about watching me hit or anything. I later found out that Sandy didn't want any other teams seeing more of me and deciding they should try and sign me. It had to be the quickest tryout in baseball history. I caught four pitches and threw once to second.

Minaya came up to me afterward and told me he'd never seen a kid throw like that before. I signed that day for $21,500. I remember I signed in the parking lot on the trunk of a car. There were no cameras or reporters. That's the way it was. It was just my father, the scouts with the Rangers, and me. The date was July 27, 1988. My life, my family's life, would never be the same. Although I certainly had bigger dreams, like playing in the big leagues and being an All-Star, the first part of my journey was now a reality. I was a professional baseball player. Yet I was still a kid in so many ways at just 16 years old.

I was both nervous and excited. I was very happy to start, but when the moment came for me to leave for Florida, I was kind of nervous because it was my first time traveling by myself. I was going to be living alone and starting my own life.

We all cried on the day I left. I remember looking back at my family during the check-in and I told myself, *Well, now you're on your own.* When that plane took off, that was it. There was no turning back. I had two suitcases, one for my clothes and one for my baseball stuff. And it was a rough trip. We were supposed to fly from San Juan to Miami, then from Miami to Sarasota, and that's where I was supposed to be picked up and driven to Port Charlotte, where spring training was taking place. Our plane out of Puerto Rico was delayed, though, so I missed the flight from Miami to Sarasota.

Since I had never flown by myself, I felt lost and didn't know what to do. I also didn't know that many people in Miami spoke Spanish, so I didn't ask anyone. Luckily, a lady who worked at the gate asked me in Spanish if I was okay. I explained everything that had happened, and she helped me find where I needed to go. The bad news was that there were no more flights going to Sarasota that day, and the next available flight wasn't until the next day at 4:00 in the afternoon. There was no alternative, so I had to sleep in the airport behind a cashier's counter with my bags. I was just lying on the carpet from about 9:30 that night until 4:00 the next day when the lady helped me book a flight to Sarasota. I had to call collect to my mom, who called Luis Rosa, who called the Rangers and told them I would be late. It was a bumpy welcome to the United States for me.

3

Living the Baseball Life

BEING AWAY FROM HOME FOR THE FIRST TIME, BEING ALONE (AT least in terms of people I knew, especially my parents) wasn't enjoyable. Playing baseball was fun. That was always fun. Learning to clean, cook, and live by myself—that was really hard at the beginning. There were many nights I spent making collect calls back to Puerto Rico, telling my parents I wanted to come home. I was homesick. Mostly, I missed all the stuff your parents do that you don't really appreciate until you have to do it yourself.

My father made it clear I wasn't coming home. Even my mother, too. They kept me strong by telling me to stay in Florida and take advantage of the opportunity I had been blessed with. They reminded me again and again that this was truly a once-in-a-lifetime chance.

I guess in many ways it was like going away to college, but the baseball season is longer than a semester. There was also no driving home to do laundry. And I was a year or two younger than the typical college freshman since I had just turned 17 a few months before arriving in Florida. Physically, I felt on par with many of the younger guys in the minor league camp. I was around 5'8" and 170 pounds, but most of my baby fat was gone. And I was quick; it was obvious from the first day that no catcher had quicker feet than me.

Besides being homesick, there was another problem. It was really difficult for me to communicate because I literally didn't speak a word of English. Well, maybe a few, but those weren't exactly conversational. There was one word I used quite frequently if I struck out or made a bad throw.

The baseball communication was a little easier. And there were players and coaches who were Hispanic and also spoke some English, so we could figure out signals and such. Trips to the mound, though, were a little more challenging at first.

I knew from the first day that I belonged, that no other catcher there could match my arm strength. My hitting wasn't turning many heads, but we all kind of knew that would come in time. All the feedback from that first camp was positive.

The Rangers' minor league system at the time did a great job of teaching the Hispanic players how to speak English. There were mandatory classes after games and workouts. And I wanted to learn. It took me just a day or two to realize that my life was going to be 100 percent easier once I could speak the same language as most of my coaches and teammates. The teacher was Nylsa Gomez, who was the wife of coach Orlando Gomez. Class was every day from 6:00 to 7:00 in the evening in a little room at a Days Inn hotel in Port Charlotte, Florida. Right after we practiced and finished our game, we had a couple hours to eat before we had to be ready for class. There were probably more than 10 players there, especially a lot of Dominican and Puerto Rican players. That helped me a lot, and Mrs. Gomez would give me extra time if I still needed help after class. She was a fantastic teacher, and we were really fortunate to have that opportunity.

Television also helped me learn the language. I'm a sports fanatic and I love to watch every sport. I really tried to understand more of the English language through sports, so I would take notes during the games and ask Mrs. Gomez about certain words. That was one of the key elements for me to learn the language quicker.

And I wasn't afraid to speak either. A lot of the younger players didn't want to look stupid or take the chance they would say the wrong word, but I wasn't shy. I just tried to get better with it each day. It was especially important at my position of catcher since I had to communicate with these American pitchers. The pitchers knew that my English wasn't good, but I had one or two words they could understand. I would also use the hand motions and body language to communicate behind the plate and help them understand what I was saying. Then when we would go back to the dugout, we would talk about it with coaches like Rudy Jaramillo or Oscar Acosta, who were both bilingual. I worked almost as hard at learning English those first few years as playing baseball. It was that important to me.

At the conclusion of camp, I was assigned to Class A Gastonia of the South Atlantic League, which meant I was skipping the rookie leagues, the lowest level of minor league baseball. I was always proud of that.

Gastonia was in North Carolina. The town had the ballpark, and that's about it. I lived with a bunch of players in an apartment we rented. It was a two-bedroom apartment for five players. During the week we would rotate the beds and the rooms. If it wasn't your day to sleep on a bed, you were going to end up sleeping on the couch or the floor. I normally slept on the couch or the floor because I wasn't comfortable sleeping on the bed. Everybody else slept there, and I just wanted to have my own space. It was actually pretty nice on the carpet, too. We'd fold up a few blankets and sleep there. I was in heaven, sleeping very well after long days at the ballpark. We had no car the first year, but there was a mall within walking distance that we would go to. There weren't a lot of food options, as this was before even the lowest rungs of the minor leagues had food spreads before and after games for players. I ate a lot of chicken nuggets and peanut butter and jelly sandwiches. When we were on the road, it was a lot of McDonald's. At the time we ordered a lot of fast food because that was the only easy thing we could order. That meant a lot of Domino's Pizza, Burger King, stuff like that. All you had to say was No. 1 or No. 2, and they would give you the meal, which made it easy.

I wasn't intimidated by anybody. I was ready to play my game, even though I was very young. The first thing that my manager Orlando Gomez let me do was call my own game. He and pitching coach Oscar Acosta never gave me the signs. I always called my own game—ever since the first inning I played in pro ball. Even before that. To me—and this was instilled by my father—calling a game was part of the catcher's job. That was my responsibility. I think it's crazy to see how many coaches nowadays, on every level from high school to college to the pros, are calling pitches. Let the catcher handle that.

That first year, really the first few years, I had to separate my offense and defense. Catching was coming naturally. That's not to say I wasn't working hard on it. It's just that my arm and my feet made me a top prospect almost immediately. Hitting was a different story. That was a process. I had trouble early with hitting because I was pulling everything to left field until Rudy Jaramillo, the roving minor league instructor who would be with me for years, started working with me. We started working in the cage, and what he told me was, "Look, you have a quick bat through the strike zone. I want you to stay inside of the ball and wait until the ball gets to you. Stay inside-out and try to hit the ball the other way." We worked on that, and I was taking extra batting practice every day. Instead of me swinging from the outside in, he taught me to go inside-out. That was my problem. My natural swing meant that I pulled the ball into left field all the time.

We had a heck of a team that first year and finished with a 92–48 record. I played the majority of our games, batting .238 with seven home runs and 42 RBIs. This was long before the philosophy of working the pitch count. I was always taught growing up to swing at a good pitch, and that never really changed over my career. During that first season, I walked just 21 times, but on the flip side, I was putting the bat on the ball. I struck out 58 times, which was the second fewest on the team among our regular starters.

Darren Oliver was the Rangers' No. 1 pitching prospect. He was a left-handed power pitcher who threw 96 to 98 miles per hour, and we moved his pitches all over the plate. He had a natural cut to his fastball. A lot of guys had trouble catching him, and I was the only one who felt comfortable because I already had great hands. So I was the one who caught all his bullpen sessions. He ended up spending 20 seasons in the big leagues as both a starter and reliever.

Another pitcher who went on to big league success—with more than 300 career saves—was Robb Nen. Back then he was a different story. He was a guy who had tremendous talent and was very good at throwing the fastball and slider. He was obviously a hard thrower, but at the time, he didn't have good control. He was a little erratic, more so than Darren. Early in his career, when I spent a few seasons with him in the minors, I had to pretty much sit in the middle of the plate so he could throw the ball right to me. They worked with him on just getting ahead in the count and making sure he threw strikes. He was throwing so hard that sometimes he didn't know where the ball was going.

There were very few people in the stands that first season at Gastonia. It was a professional league, but it didn't feel like it. It was an old ballpark, and I remember the light standards were made out of wood. The clubhouse was probably as big as a living room. It was a season of learning for me, knowing that I had never been away from home before. What I was most proud of was that I was able to survive being away from my parents for the first time. My father came to visit once, but that was it.

After working on my swing all season in Gastonia, I headed to play winter ball for the first time. Well, I guess I had played winter ball in Puerto Rico growing up, but that was because we always played baseball, no matter the season. I didn't play much my first two years as a pro in winter ball, which wasn't a surprise since I was by far the youngest player on the team. I was the bullpen catcher the first year and third-string the year after that.

So I used those two winters to work on my hitting. I would just come out to the ballpark early and work. In Puerto Rico all we used were aluminum bats. The first time I held a wooden bat was at the baseball academy a few years earlier. That was a big adjustment, of course, because aluminum is lighter than wood. And sometimes the weight distribution was all over the place with aluminum. On the other hand, if you didn't cup a wooden bat, the weight would be on the sweet spot. But if you cupped the end, the weight was more evenly distributed.

I remember they gave me two bats when I arrived at spring training that first year. The two bats they gave me were 34-inch, 32-ounces, and I used that size my entire career. I never changed. I was one of the players who owned more bats than anybody. I don't know why that was. I might practice with different models, but once the game started it was a 34-inch, 32-ounce double-dipped bat from Louisville Slugger.

The following year, in 1990, I was promoted to high Class A Port Charlotte of the Florida State League, which was cool and convenient since that's where the team's spring training and minor league headquarters were based.

I made the All-Star team and was a better player because of all the work I had put in during the offseason. I really used winter ball in Puerto Rico to work on a lot of things since I wasn't playing too much. I didn't have to think about catching or calling the game. Instead, I could just focus on my hitting. I used to wake up early every day and run for miles, as if I were preparing myself for a marathon. I would run with some friends that I grew up with, and we would go for 15 miles one day and 20 miles a few days after that—from my town to the next town to the next town and back. I stopped that after a month because I knew it was not the right workout for my position, but I loved running. I guess in some ways it helped build up endurance in the legs. That's kind of like how pitchers or even boxers do a lot of running, but I also needed to save my knees. Too much running is not a good thing when you are squatting for four or five hours a day.

Running would be part of my morning workout, and then in the afternoon, I would go to the local gym in my hometown and lift weights. That was the first time I really dedicated myself to lifting. My future manager with the Rangers, Bobby Valentine, came to visit me that offseason. He spent three days in Puerto Rico just to work out with me at the gym. I'm sure he just wanted to develop our relationship, too, and see where I was from. That was cool. It meant a lot to me as a young kid.

I can't stress this enough: back in my era, the one thing they emphasized, at least in the Rangers organization, was to be aggressive at the plate. And I was extremely aggressive, even more so that second season.

I walked 12 times in 432 plate appearances in the Florida State League, but I still raised my batting average by 50 points and had seven triples. I had great plate coverage. I could hit balls that were way outside. I've always been a good bad-ball hitter—ever since I was a young kid playing in the youth leagues. And I try to teach that. Sometimes I tell younger players they shouldn't try to be too perfect. Your bat head can reach pretty far outside, and you can still hit the ball in the gap.

Just look at Vladimir Guerrero, who should be inducted to the Hall of Fame in 2018 after coming just 15 votes shy of joining my class. He had himself an incredible career hitting balls way out of the strike zone. He even hit a few that bounced first and he finished with a .318 career batting average and 449 home runs. Pretty sure anyone would take those numbers.

The only negative thing about my game at the time was that I was still pulling everything. When I started working with Rudy, he was extremely positive about my batting while also encouraging me to swing inside-out. "Look, I don't want you to change your aggressiveness as a hitter," he said. "I want you to stay the way you are and keep swinging." He was trying to get me to drive the ball the other way instead of pulling it all the time. So I worked on that in Puerto Rico and then I came to Port Charlotte and had a pretty decent season offensively. But the Rangers didn't care about my hitting. They found out that I was a major league prospect because of my catching.

One thing I remember is that other teams didn't run much on me in the minor leagues. They knew that I had a good arm. I was able to throw out the majority of runners who did try to steal on me, so that's why they didn't run much. Even sometimes with a full count on the batter, they didn't go. They just stayed on first base.

I never paid attention to whether the Rangers thought of me as a top prospect or not. Looking back, I obviously was. I skipped rookie ball and was in high Class A at 18 years old, which is unheard of. Heck, I was so young that I had never shaved before. I was a second-year pro ballplayer before I even shaved. I looked so young that security sometimes wouldn't let me in or thought I was the batboy.

At the time, though, I just knew that they treated me well and worked with me all the time to get better. I never felt like I was set apart from the rest of my teammates. I always stayed humble, just trying to do my job in the minors and make my ultimate dream come true.

My footwork and release behind the plate came naturally, and my good arm made everything happen. My height was perfect. At that point I was fully grown and stood around 5'9", maybe half an inch shorter. I wasn't 6'2" or 6'4", and that was an advantage. It helped me to stay low and be quicker. I was so quick that I wouldn't even feel myself making the throws around the bases. It was like instinct. I would stay right down there and just let the ball go. When I was a kid in Puerto Rico, I used to throw tennis balls against a concrete wall. Throw it, make the catch, and do the footwork. That helped me to make sure I had the muscle memory down. I would do that for hours.

Plus, I was blessed with a great arm. It even drew some comments from my own pitchers. When I threw the ball to second base, they had to move from the pitching rubber because if they didn't move I might hit them right in the stomach. Yes, the gut, not the head. That's how low the ball went as it passed the mound on the way to second base. I remember one time when I was catching Josh Beckett with the Florida Marlins, and a runner tried to steal. Josh had a tendency to bend down and stay close to the rubber when somebody was running, and this time the ball almost hit him. It was a perfect throw right there at the knees of the second baseman, and the runner was out by five feet. But Josh looked at me like I had scared him. I told him that he needed to move next time. He definitely learned his lesson because he never did it again.

Off the field, life in Port Charlotte was a lot better than Gastonia. We had an ocean, and I think water is always a peaceful thing. It was five or six guys living together again, but this time we were in a bigger place, a four-bedroom house. Jose Hernandez, who went on to have a solid 15-year big-league career, was my roommate. We lived like a mile and a half from the ballpark and during the season we decided to buy a car. It was an old Oldsmobile in very bad shape, just a car to get back and forth. That car always had a problem, and a lot of times, the brakes would go out. Jose was the only one of us who had a license, so he always drove the car. He would say, "Here we go, the brakes are out again. So hold on." He would use the gears to bring the speed down and bring it back up and, if we still had some speed by the time we got to the ballpark, we'd end up crashing into the trees. Then Jose would put the car in reverse and slowly back up to the ballpark. It's a funny story today, but it was scary at the time.

I also started to cook. I'm a good cook now because of that. I remember that I called my mom collect two or three times a week for cooking advice. I would make white rice, red beans, chicken stew, beef stew, whatever. And I had to walk from the house to the supermarket, which was a mile or so away. Then I had to walk back with all the food I had just bought. After catching nine innings and going to the store, by the time I got to the house sometimes I was already tired. So I would end up not cooking, just eating a sandwich instead. But when I was cooking, I would call my mother and say, "Mom, how do I do this? What do I need to put on this?" I learned to cook very quickly. That was a lot better than all those Chicken McNuggets I had been eating.

By the next season at Double A Tulsa, I was having a good year. I was 19 years old. And Geno Petralli was having a great year for the Rangers with Mike Stanley as the backup catcher. So I thought I was still a couple levels away from heading to the majors, that I would go to Triple A first. I was just thinking about having another great season and learning more, being a better player in a better league. I, however, didn't start the season well at all. I think I was hitting .200 after the first month. I had no idea at the time, but my life was about to dramatically change. And not just because I was less than two months away from getting married.

4

Bound for the Big Leagues

ATHLETES ARE ALWAYS TALKING ABOUT BEING FOCUSED ON THE task at hand, taking it day-to-day, not looking ahead. And as boring as it sounds, that mentality really allows one to stay on task. No reason to worry about two months from now when it's impossible to know what the circumstances are going to be. Today we have a baseball game, so let's focus on that.

So when I tell you being promoted from Double A to the Texas Rangers was the last thing on my mind, trust me it was. First off 99.9 percent of players who eventually play Major League Baseball progress through the minor leagues one step at a time: rookie ball, short-season Class A, Class A, high Class A, Double A, and finally Triple A. And it's usually not a quick process either, as some guys spend five or six years working their way up.

My thinking was I would spend all of 1991 with Tulsa and then maybe start the following year with our Triple A affiliate, which at the time was Oklahoma City. Obviously, like for any minor leaguer, playing with the Rangers was the ultimate goal, the ultimate dream, but I just didn't think that day was close.

What was close was my wedding to Maribel Rivera. In fact, we had the rehearsal on the field on June 19. The plan was for us to marry in between games of a doubleheader the following day.

Maribel grew up in New York and then moved to Puerto Rico as a teenager. We started dating when I was 15, although she told people she didn't like me at first because I was too quiet. I, though, didn't take no for an answer. I kept bugging her about going out with me. When her grandmother died, I spent a lot of time with her through that stretch, and that was kind of the turning point. We were always a couple after that.

When I left for spring training in 1991, we had been together for more than three years and we were already talking about marriage. We were young, but we loved each other very much and knew we wanted to have kids and raise a family. We couldn't have been more in tune with what our futures would hold.

Here's kind of a crazy story. Before I left Puerto Rico that offseason, Maribel asked me if she could come visit me after school ended in June. She was a senior in high school. She wanted to make sure it wouldn't be a distraction, and I told her it wouldn't be. So I left her some money to buy plane tickets for her and her mother to come see me for a week in Tulsa.

In mid-May she called me and said, "I bought my own ticket and I'm leaving." And I said, "But where are you going? Back to New York?" She said, "No, I'm going to Tulsa. I'm going to be with you." I asked her if she was sure she wanted to come, and she said, "Yes, I'm already committed. I'm ready. I've got everything planned. And I'll arrive at 11:45 tomorrow night."

And there she was, walking through the airport gate at 11:45 the next night. And we went home, back to the place I was renting. That next day, everybody started calling me from Puerto Rico, saying that nobody knew where Maribel was. Everyone was scared. Her mother and the rest of her family were going crazy since they couldn't find her. I talked to my dad, and he could tell by my voice that something was up. He said, "If she's there, you'd better tell me that she's there, so I'll know she's okay. But you need to tell me the truth." And I said, "Yeah, she's right here. She left home to stay with me and didn't tell anyone." We were already planning the ceremony at that point.

On June 20, the day we were slated to be married, I was batting .274, which was a huge improvement from flirting with the Mendoza Line that first month. I was never a great hitter in the cold weather. Not many of us from Puerto Rico are since we are just used to the warmer conditions.

My manager, Bobby Jones (who had also managed me at Port Charlotte), called me in that afternoon before batting practice. I went into Bobby's office, and he said, "I have to ask you a couple of things: do you want to get married and stay here in Tulsa? Or do you want to play in the big leagues?" I said, "What do you mean? Of course I want to play in the big leagues." He said, "Alright, then you're out of the lineup. They called you up. You've got to be in Chicago tomorrow. You need to talk to your girlfriend because you can't get married. You guys have got to go." And I said, "No problem, no problem."

Looking back, it seems like others were expecting this more than I was, even though I was going to be the youngest player in the big leagues. "Everybody knows he is a franchise player. I have never seen a catcher at any minor league level as good," Jones told *The Dallas Morning News* on June 16, 1991. "It's only a matter of time before the call comes to send him on. He is the quickest I have ever seen in getting the ball from his mitt to his throwing hand. No one runs on him. And he calls a great game. Pitchers shake off his signs maybe once a game. When he is catching, you don't have to worry about pitchouts or passed balls. He is in total control from the time he puts on the mask."

I was shocked because I hadn't been thinking about whether they were going to call me up or not. I was so focused on what I was doing in Tulsa because I was having a good year and had the everyday job. When they gave me the news, I thought I was dreaming. I actually asked Bobby Jones to repeat himself. And I asked Oscar Acosta, who was our pitching coach, to come in and tell me in Spanish just to make sure I wasn't missing something. He smiled and said, "You're going to the big leagues!"

My father and my brother were there visiting for the week, so they were already at the ballpark. They had come to Tulsa for the wedding and to see a few games. I brought them down from the bleachers and I said, "Well, I've got to go to Chicago. They called me up—I'm a big leaguer!" They were happy, and we all hugged, although they had to stay there for two more days waiting for their flight back to Puerto Rico. I was already in Chicago by the time they left Tulsa.

I always appreciated that the Rangers and general manager Tom Grieve gave me the choice of staying for a day and being married or flying immediately to Chicago. Maribel wasn't thrilled with postponing the wedding, but she was also completely supportive of my decision.

There has also been a lot of confusion over the years on when we were officially married. *The New York Times* and other newspapers ran stories about how we married that morning at the Tulsa courthouse before I flew out. That's not how it happened. We ended up being married the following spring training in Port Charlotte. We didn't do anything in Tulsa. I have no idea where that story came from, but it became gospel thereafter.

Maribel and I flew to Chicago, and, despite having slept maybe two hours the night before, I was too excited to close my eyes on the flight. We arrived at the team hotel in the late afternoon, and within seconds I was on my way to Comiskey

Park. This was turning out to be quite the day. Maribel had no idea how to find the ballpark so she stayed at the hotel.

I didn't expect to play that night in Chicago. Think about my previous day—waking up, thinking I'm going to be married and playing a doubleheader in Tulsa, then having to go from the ballpark to the airport. I flew in, went to the team hotel and then from the hotel to the ballpark. Some of the coaches were waiting for me in the lobby. They wanted to make sure I got from the hotel to Comiskey Park early. Once I got to the park, Bobby Valentine said, "Welcome. You're in the lineup. You're playing, hitting ninth."

Wait, what?

The Rangers' longtime, legendary radio announcer Eric Nadel approached me after batting practice about doing a quick interview for the pregame show. I said yes, which really showed how far my English had come along in just two years. Maribel spoke English, having grown up mostly in New York, so we would talk all the time. I guess that was practice, much like working on my hitting. She would correct me if I said something the wrong way when we were talking in English.

I wasn't afraid to speak English, and that's the way to do it. If you're afraid, or if you're trying to speak English but still think in Spanish, then speaking in English is probably not going to work. Just make sure to be you, the person you can be. And I did that. I didn't want to ask for help translating. I knew that if I kept asking for help, I would never get better.

It was so important for me to learn the language because I knew it would help my ability as a player, as a catcher, and as a hitter. It would speed things up and it would improve my communication with the pitcher, though there wasn't too much shaking me off when I was behind the plate. Even Nolan Ryan didn't shake me off much.

The final question that Nadel asked me was whether Valentine told me that I was only there for two weeks until Geno Petralli came off the disabled list. My answer: "That's what they told me. But I'm never going back."

I'm pretty sure no one would have imagined at the time of that interview that we would both end up honored by the Baseball Hall of Fame. (Nadel received the Ford C. Frick award in 2014 for broadcasting excellence.)

Petralli, 31 years old at the time of my promotion, was the starting catcher for the majority of the four seasons before my arrival. He was a solid big league backstop. Stanley was a few years younger and later in his career was an All-Star with the New York Yankees. He could hit and he ended up with almost 200 career home runs. They, more or less, were a platoon with Petralli facing right-handed starting pitchers, and Stanley facing lefties.

Although the majority of my new teammates were strangers, outside of maybe seeing them at spring training, there was a familiar face—that of Juan "Igor" Gonzalez, who was also from Vega Baja. He was a couple years older, but we played against each other growing up. Igor was a power-hitting outfielder who was in the midst of a breakout season with 27 home runs and 102 RBIs. And he was just getting started.

The day Gonzalez signed with the Rangers, I was at the park and I told him someday we were going to play together in the big leagues. I would check out the box scores in the newspapers at the minor league clubhouses and I would always look at what Igor did first.

TITO RODRIGUEZ
OLDER BROTHER

"There was this big series in our hometown, Ivan's team against Juan's team. I think Ivan was nine, so Juan was probably 11 years old. They played a doubleheader on a Saturday, and in the first game, Ivan pitched and shut them out 1–0. They couldn't hit him. I think he had 20 strikeouts in seven innings. Then in the second game, Juan pitched and he won 1–0. That was a special day. It was obvious those two were destined to do great things in baseball. I've never seen so many fans come to watch a little league game before or since. Everyone wanted to see them play each other. It's incredible to think about, these two kids from a small town in Puerto Rico playing together for the same major league team. What are the chances of that?"

Kevin Brown was on the mound for my first game with the Rangers. He ended up winning more than 200 games in the big leagues and was one of the better right-handed pitchers of his era. We worked really well together. Kevin was a guy who was quick to the plate, which helped me get a quick release. The first guy I threw out was Joey Cora, who stole 117 bases in the big leagues. I threw him out by 10 feet. Our second baseman Julio Franco caught the ball perfectly and waited for Cora to arrive kind of like in that scene from *Major League*—minus the middle finger. Then Julio looked at me after he flipped the ball to the shortstop, as if to say, *Are you kidding me, kid? Is that for real?* I guess he never saw a catcher throw down to second base at 92 miles per hour.

Three innings later, for reasons I've never been entirely sure of, Warren Newson got on base and tried stealing second. The result was the same.

Entering the top of the ninth, we were trailing 3–2. The White Sox closer was Bobby Thigpen, who set a record with 57 saves the season before. He was unable to finish us off, as Ruben Sierra, our All-Star right fielder from Puerto Rico, and Franco each hit home runs.

Melido Perez then came in to pitch for the White Sox. We had runners on second and third with two outs. And I was at the plate. Roughly 12 hours earlier, I walked into the park in Tulsa thinking it was my wedding day. Now here I was, at one of the most historic ballparks in the history of the game, and the count was two balls and a strike.

I hit a line drive in the gap of right-center field, and both runs scored. My first hit. My first two RBIs. An incredible moment standing on first base. Someone was smart enough to ask for the baseball, which I greatly appreciated because I was in shock at the moment. I still have the ball, too. After the third out, I was walking back to the dugout and I noticed no one was running onto the field for the bottom of the ninth. They were waiting for me, to shake my hand, give me high fives, and hug me. It was a moment that will live with me forever. We won the game 7–3.

After the game all the media came into the clubhouse. I had just showered and came back to my locker with a towel around me. My clothes were gone, which I guess was a little rookie hazing from some of the veteran players. I saw that there were three female reporters standing there, so, of course, I was shy talking to them like that. I was definitely embarrassed. Still, it was a magical day.

Luckily, I was able to grab a few hours of sleep before heading back to the ballpark the following day. That Friday night we played a four-hour, 11-inning game against the White Sox. Once again,

I was starting and batting ninth. I had another hit, too. This time around Chicago decided not to run on me.

My big memory from that game, though, was who our starting pitcher was: Nolan Ryan. This was ridiculous. I grew up watching him striking everyone out. He still holds the major league record with seven no-hitters and 5,714 career strikeouts. Nolan was 44 years old, and I was 19. I guess that was a first in big league history, a 40-year-old throwing to a teenager.

We went to meet with the pitching coach, Tom House, and go over the scouting reports. Nolan said to Tom, "Don't worry about those. There's no need." He looked at me and said, "Pudge, put some fingers down, and I'll throw it." I knew he was a power pitcher, so the main fingers I put down were for fastballs. He ended up throwing 85 or 90 percent fastballs that night and he allowed just one hit.

I really went out of my way to call for a lot of fastballs in and I realized that's what he liked. So one of my first signals was for that pitch, no matter what the situation was. Whether or not there were runners on, whatever the pitch count was, it didn't matter—just throw that inside fastball. He didn't shake me off. He said early on in that game, "When I'm not making any signal or movement toward you, it's the same pitch, just change locations." I picked it up really quick. I would go fastball in, stay there, then go out for a pitch. Just let him throw the heat and change up where I put my glove.

He was old enough that he could have been my father. And looking back, he was like a father to me. We spent a lot of time just talking about pitchers and their mind-set. The advice he gave me, the questions he answered for me, those stayed with me throughout the next 20 years. There's no way I become the catcher I did without having Nolan around those first few seasons.

Following that first game, he said, "That's the kid I want behind the plate, and I want to throw to him every time."

That meant the world to me. Heck, it still does.

I grew up with a bunch of veteran players like Nolan, Brown, Dean Palmer, Kenny Rogers, Franco, Steve Buechele, Sierra, and Stanley, who, in particular, taught me and helped me a lot. He could have felt angriness or bitterness since he wasn't catching much anymore, but instead he picked me up and took me under his wing. I remembered that later in my career and I always worked with the younger guys even if they were trying to take my job. That lesson came from Mike.

Those guys, by both example and through their words, were my education, my introduction to what it meant to be a big leaguer. They taught me how to carry myself, how to treat the fans and media with respect. And to always play hard. What I really appreciated those first few years was that they didn't treat me like a kid. I was on the team, so I was expected to do my job just like everyone else. They treated me like an adult. I was incredibly fortunate to be put in that position, to be around the first-class ballplayers that were on those Rangers teams.

KENNY ROGERS
RANGERS PITCHER

"When Pudge first got here, we knew just how good of a player he was from the get-go. He was far better than the catchers we had ever thrown to or seen. All we had to do was focus on making good pitches and understanding what we wanted to do. It simplified pitching for us, which is a huge benefit.

"Even at 19 his talent was undeniable. Without a doubt, when they brought him up, he wasn't going to sit. And

when you were starting as a pitcher, you wanted him to be catching because of all the things he brought to the table. Talent-wise, I don't know of any catcher who could do as much or the same kinds of things. You look at everybody else; he was far superior. If you needed a home run, he could hit one. If you needed him to throw out a runner, he'd throw them out. I mean, if there was a way to do it, I'm sure he would have found a way to throw a guy out at home plate, on his own."

My rookie season went pretty well. We finished 85–77, in third place in the American League West. I played in 88 games, batted .264 and finished fourth in the American League Rookie of the Year voting. The award was won by Minnesota second baseman Chuck Knoblauch, who played in 151 games. I threw out nearly half of those trying to steal against me (34-of-70), and that 49 percent caught-stealing percentage led the league for catchers who played in at least half their team's games.

There was a lot of room to grow, however. I didn't hit my first home run until my 59th game—on August 30 against Kansas City Royals pitcher Storm Davis at Arlington Stadium—and finished the year with just three. And my plate discipline, well, let's just say it wasn't a strength. I walked just five times in 288 plate appearances. Still, how many people accomplish their childhood dream before turning 20 years old? I was incredibly fortunate. Know what else? I proved to myself that I could play with these guys at the highest level. And at that point, there was no ceiling to what I could accomplish.

5

Breaking In

ONE OF THE MORE COMMON QUESTIONS I'VE BEEN ASKED OVER the years is: who is the best pitcher I ever caught. And from my rookie season until the last time I squatted behind the dish, I've always said the same man. His name is Nolan Ryan.

Yeah, I knew all about him before that first time I caught him in my second big league game. Plus, he was in the Rangers organization even when I was in the minor leagues. I would see him pitch in spring training when I was in minor league camp. We always loved to go watch the big league games and we would try to get all our work done early so we could leave by 1:00 PM to see them. They had a picnic area around the bullpen at our spring training complex in Port Charlotte, Florida, so when Nolan was warming up I was always there. And I always listened to him when he talked about what he liked to do, be it pitching or working out. Heck, anything Nolan said was like gospel for me.

When I first came up, I knew he was going to be one of my pitchers and I looked at him like any other pitcher. I wasn't really intimidated by the thought of catching him. I mean he was older than I was and had been in baseball for more than 20 years by the time I was there, but the good thing was that we clicked very quickly. I started doing things behind the plate that he really liked, and that's why we worked so well together.

Nolan is a very quiet person, but at the same time, if you asked him a question, he would always take the time to answer, to try and help. He taught me so much about pitching and even about catching.

When we played together, he was always very serious and professional about going through his workouts. Sometimes we wouldn't see him. He was at the ballpark, but he spent a ton of time on the stationary bike. He would ride that for an hour and a half or two hours, then go to the gym, and then go out on the field. By the time he got out there, we were already stretching and taking batting practice. In old Arlington Stadium, he always came in from right field to shag balls and he did his running there on the warning track. And then he would come back in and go to the bike. Finally, when the game started, he would come out and sit down. I would have some conversations with him, but not too many because he was so focused. That's true even during games he wasn't pitching. He was so intense, and that's definitely a trait I tried to emulate.

Being a young player, I noticed all the extra work he was putting in at 43, 44, 45 years old. Think about this: less than 1 percent of 1 percent of major league ballplayers are still out there at 40. I didn't play a game in my 40s. And Nolan didn't even come to the Rangers until he was 42. Then he pitched long enough to have his numbered retired by the team. That's ridiculous. He struck out nearly 1,000 hitters with the Rangers and tossed two no-hitters. It's just incredible to think about.

Back then we were all working out hard, going to the gym and doing the things we had to do to keep ourselves in shape. When I came up in 1991, I would see players like Nolan, Julio Franco, Ruben Sierra, Juan Gonzalez, Kevin Brown, Kenny Rogers, guys who were always in the gym, working out and lifting weights.

That was a team that knew how important it was to stay in shape. And that's why we played so well.

The final game Nolan pitched—at Seattle on September 22, 1993—it was obvious he was having a tough time. He kept looking at our manager, Bobby Valentine, in the dugout. He was walking around too much, and I knew that something wasn't right. So, I went out to the mound and asked him, "Are you okay?" He said, "I'm tired."

His right throwing elbow was also hurting, and we learned after the game that he had suffered a torn ulnar lateral ligament a few batters earlier. He was just wild and all over the place with his pitches. He walked four of the last six batters he faced.

Then Bobby came out, Nolan handed him the ball, and this legend, this man I had so much admiration for—still do to this very day—was done. We were watching him walk off the field, which a manager and catcher never do, but this was different. We knew this was it. Father Time remains undefeated, though maybe in Nolan's case it was a draw because he was 46 at this point. I was elected to the Baseball Hall of Fame a couple months after turning 45, and Nolan was incredibly still pitching at that age. Just five days before that last start, he didn't allow an earned run over seven innings against the California Angels.

What was cool was that the opposing crowd was giving him a beautiful standing ovation, saying thank you for his unmatched career. Nolan was walking back to the dugout, and at The Kingdome, the Mariners' old stadium, there were no steps. It was just straight in. The door leading back to the clubhouse was in the middle of the dugout, so everybody was outside there shaking his hand. But he didn't stay long. He went right to the clubhouse.

It was tough. It's sad to see people like that walking away. That's why when I retired, I knew that I could play a few more years, but I didn't want to get to that point. Nolan played for 27 seasons and retired at 46 years old. Are you kidding me? He pitched from 1966 to 1993 and he was still throwing 96 or 97 at the end. There will never be another Nolan Ryan. For me, though, he's a great man and friend before anything else.

Those first few seasons with the Rangers, we had quite the pitching staff, we really did. Nolan, Kevin, Jose Guzman, and Bobby Witt. Kenny at that point mostly came out of the bullpen, but he'd make some spot starts here and there. Jeff Russell was an All-Star closer. Imagine that group. That's a staff any team in baseball would take. I had to be at the top of my game for those guys to be comfortable with a young kid catching them.

With Kevin, if you didn't know how to catch that sinker—we're talking one of the nastiest sinkers the game has ever seen—you were going to have a broken thumb. That sinker would move in ways that defied physics. After a few games together, it wasn't that difficult for me, but you saw the trouble that pitch gave catchers and hitters over the remainder of his career.

Thinking of all the pitchers that I caught, early on and later in my career, the good thing was that they felt comfortable with me behind the plate. There is nothing more important to a catcher. I certainly wasn't perfect and sometimes I did things I wasn't supposed to, but at the same time, I tried to do my best to help them. I've always said—and I believe every catcher should have this mentality—I'd rather help a pitcher succeed than hit a thousand home runs. To me, calling a great game and helping a pitcher be at his very best is what being a catcher is all about.

Early in my second season with the Rangers, on April 17, 1992, to be exact, I had one of those welcome-to-the-big-leagues moments. In some ways you really aren't a major league catcher until Rickey Henderson tries to steal a base on you. That is Rickey

Henderson, the greatest leadoff hitter to ever play the game. He stole 1,406 bases in his career, and no one else even sniffed 1,000. Rickey led the American League in steals 11 of 12 years from 1980 to 1991, including a ridiculous 130 in 1982. That's three more than I had my entire career, and only five catchers in baseball history stole more bags than I did.

Rickey actually stole second off me late in my rookie season, so this wasn't the first time he tried to run. It was the seventh inning, and we were beating the Oakland A's 6–5. There were two outs and runners at the corners with Rickey at first. Kevin was pitching for us. I was fully expecting him to run on the first pitch, and there went Rickey with a pretty good jump, too. My throw, which was clocked at 93 miles per hour, beat him to second base and ended the inning. If my throw wasn't perfect, he would have been safe. Henderson slid into second baseman Jeff Huson's glove as the ball arrived. We won the game by a run.

The next day, as I was finishing batting practice, Rickey walked up to the cage and said, "I owe you one, you know that? I owe you a big one. Don't be doing that to me too often now."

At that point I had thrown out eight of the last 10 guys who tried to steal on me. My arm never felt better. This is how Manager Valentine described my 1992 performance against Oakland at the time: "You see it coming. It was the best against the best. All I saw was a bullet, a laser. It looked like smoke was coming out of the back of the ball. I think he could make the All-Star Game this year with his defense alone. He blocks the ball in the dirt as well as anyone I've ever seen."

As a catcher, as any athlete I would think, you want to challenge yourself against the best, and Rickey was the best. He stole nine bases off me, and I was fortunate enough to throw him out a few times over the years. Rickey didn't run much against me, though, and at one point he even went eight years without attempting a theft with me behind the plate. Rickey is among those iconic players that I'm so honored to join as a first-ballot Hall of Fame selection. He was fun to compete against.

That same year as my epic mano-a-mano with Rickey, I was named to my first All-Star Game in 1992 as a reserve. The game was played at Jack Murphy Stadium in San Diego, which was cool because this was before interleague play. Although I wasn't Johnny Bench at the plate, my offense was showing gradual improvement. By season's end my numbers included a .260 batting average and eight home runs. I also increased my on-base percentage 24 points from my rookie season by showing a little more plate discipline. And the 116 games I caught were the fourth most in baseball history for a player age 20 or younger. Also, I won my first Gold Glove, throwing out 52 percent of would-be base stealers.

RANGERS MANAGER
BOBBY VALENTINE

"He took such pride in his work behind the plate. Nothing got by him. And when guys got on base, he made it a personal challenge to stop the running. Early on, guys knew he was young, knew he was breaking in, and they challenged him.

"He could really hit. He was as good a breaking ball hitter as there ever has been. He could run, steal a base. He learned to hit with power, too. There's really nothing he couldn't do on a ball field."

There were two other major storylines that season. On August 31 in one of the biggest trades in baseball history at the time, we sent Ruben Sierra, our three-time All-Star right fielder;

starting pitcher Bobby Witt; and closer Jeff Russell to Oakland for Jose Canseco, the 1988 American League MVP and probably the most recognizable name and face in the game. There were always cameras following Jose, who did nothing to shy away from the fame. We were really opposites on that front because I just wanted to play baseball and go home to my family. No partying and nightclubs for me.

Know what, though, Jose was a good teammate. He came in and went about his business and he was very professional. I don't think I can say anything bad about him. He was a guy who would always come in and get dressed, grab his bat, and go to the cages. That's what he loved to do. He didn't go and practice in the outfield; that wasn't his thing. He just wanted to hit baseballs, and, in terms of hitting them far, I'm not sure anyone did it better. Maybe Mark McGwire. Babe Ruth was a little before my time, but I'm guessing he hit some long ones, too.

Jose always had a bat and was always in the video room, studying pitches, watching the pitcher and what he did, checking out the rotation of the ball, and things like that. When he was in the dugout, he was watching every single pitch the pitcher threw. He really, really paid attention to the game of baseball.

That's why he was such a good power hitter because, I think, he was looking for pitches when he was batting. And when he was looking for a certain pitch, and they threw it, he didn't miss it. I've never seen a guy who swung that hard in my career. And in batting practice he always put on a show. Everybody stopped doing what they were doing to watch him hit balls out of the ballpark. He was good with everybody and talked to everyone.

As we touched upon in the first chapter, I was shocked when his book came out. And it wasn't only me; it was everybody. We never thought that he would do something like that because we played with him. There's a brotherhood. There's a kinship. Never mind making up what he knows to be boldface lies, but just trying to harm your former teammates' reputations, I couldn't imagine doing that, no matter the circumstances.

His teammates—who played with him in Oakland, with the Rangers, and all the other organizations—I think their reaction was the same as mine. I don't know why he wrote that. It was very painful. To see him, a player that we respected on the field and in the clubhouse, do something like that, it hurt. And he was great with the fans, a guy who would go out and sign autographs. It was shocking. Up until then, Jose Canseco made baseball a better game, and I had a lot of respect and admiration for him.

When the book came out in 2005, I think those of us still playing just felt like: look, we can't let him affect our job or our focus, and there's really no reason to think about it. I have nothing to hide, and, if people want to believe a guy like that, I mean, there's nothing you can do. It was time to move on, continue playing, and being the best teammate I could be.

I think I've seen him once since then—at an event with a lot of players. What was I going to do, turn my back on him? If he comes to shake my hand, I'm not going to leave him hanging. I'm not that kind of person. He knew what he did, and we knew what he did. But that was his decision, you know? I think it was a charity event or something like that. We were all part of the group, and I saw a lot of people turning away from him. And it's sad to see that. I think there are better ways to make money than to trash your former teammates and friends, but that's not my call.

Although Jose didn't even play 200 games with us in Texas, he left quite the legacy, throwing out his arm while pitching the ninth inning of a blowout at Fenway Park and missing the last three months of the season and, of course, having that fly ball bounce off his head and go into the stands for a home run. I have never seen either of those instances happen before or since. Canseco was a heck of a hitter, though, and finished with 462 home runs. After a disappointing 45–41 start, Bobby V. was let go as our manager. What was amazing looking back was that he was just 42 at the time and was in his eighth season as the Rangers' skipper. Nolan was three years older than our manager.

Bobby was a well-respected guy. He gave me the opportunity to play in the big leagues. He and general manager Tom Grieve called me up. I owe them both a lot because Tom made the decision to call me up, and Bobby made the decision to put me in the lineup. And he let me play my game. He was never on me, never talked to me about doing this or doing that. He just let me do my job, and that's one of the things that I loved about him. He gave me the green light from Day One.

He told me right away, "You're going to be the everyday catcher, and when you need a day off, you let me know." But I would never really ask for a day off. They put me right in there and just let me call my own game, play my own game, offensively and defensively. He never said anything bad to me. He was just shaking my hand, telling me great job.

They don't let catchers today call their games like I did. Sometimes I see a catcher looking into the dugout. And I'm like, *I can't believe I'm seeing this.* All the high school and college coaches are calling pitches. Stop it. Let the catchers call the game because they know what pitches are working. And it would speed the games up, too.

After Toby Harrah, a former Rangers infielder, finished the 1992 season as manager, Kevin Kennedy was named the permanent replacement. Kevin's a very funny, happy man. He was always keeping the team loose and he was one of the better managers that I played for during my career. We talked a lot—in part because he was a minor league catcher before going into coaching. We sat down and chatted during the games, in between innings. When our team was hitting, he would sit down with me and talk about things that he saw. And he would ask me about why certain things happened in the game. Kevin was a fantastic communicator, one of the best I encountered in baseball. He wasn't just that way with me; he was like that with everybody.

We were an improved team in 1993 and went 86–76, which was one shy of the second most wins in franchise history, going way back to 1961 when they were the Washington Senators. We had quite the offense that year. Dean Palmer, Rafael Palmeiro, and Juan combined for 116 home runs with my hometown pal, "Igor," leading the league for the second straight season; this time he hit 46.

As for me I was coming along at the plate and set career highs across the board, batting .273 with 10 home runs and 66 RBIs. I also had 28 doubles and four triples. Not only did I steal my first career base, I also finished with eight. They might call me Pudge, but I could run a little.

The 1993 season was my last with my wonderful teammate, Julio, who left as a free agent. He ended up outlasting even Nolan, which I thought was impossible, but Franco played until he was 48 years old in 2007. I'm sure everyone has heard of the term "natural hitter," one of those guys who could roll out of bed, be handed a bat, and drill a line drive up the middle. That was Julio.

Julio invited me to his house when I was a young player. He was always very accommodating and would invite us to the house and have dinner. He was 13 years older than I was, so he was a mentor figure. He talked to me about the game, and on the field during batting practice, I always loved to hit with his group. I would take ground balls in the infield or go to second base where he was and take ground balls with him. And we talked.

He taught me a lot. He made me into a mature player very quickly. He taught me how to be a player like him, even though I was still a teenager when I was called up. He talked to me like a man. He said, "You are one of us. You are not a kid anymore. You are a major league catcher, so you have to play like a major league catcher, even though you're 19. That's just a number. You've got to come and do your job." There were no excuses. That's one of the reasons I was so incredibly fortunate to play in the Rangers organization at that time, to have a guy like Julio watching out for me.

By the time he left, it was after my third season when I was 21, and I was a solid veteran because of his influence. I knew what I needed to do. I could still joke around and have fun at the right moment, but when it came time for baseball, I was all business. I was extremely serious. And a big reason why was because of Julio. He's a lifelong friend.

Let's see, is there anything else worth mentioning during the 1993 season? I won my second Gold Glove, I started my first All-Star Game, Nolan pitched his final game, Juan hit a lot of home runs, and that about covers it.

Just kidding.

In some ways it's disappointing that the first memory many people have of Nolan and Robin Ventura is when the Chicago White Sox third baseman charged the mound on August 4, 1993. We're talking about one of the greatest pitchers to ever take the hill and we're talking about a guy who finished his career with nearly 2,000 hits and 300 home runs. He also won six Gold Gloves.

Honestly, I probably shouldn't have even been on the field that night. Less than a week earlier, Hubie Brooks of the Kansas City Royals mistakenly hit the side of my face on his backswing, which fractured my left cheekbone. I had surgery the next day and was supposed to miss six weeks. Instead, I missed three games. It was different back then. Today, I would have been placed on the disabled list without anyone even talking with me. Then, they came to me after the surgery and said, "How do you feel?" I said, "I'm good," and that was that. I was back in the lineup. My first game back, I left after six innings because of dizziness and headaches. I took the next day off and was back in the lineup with Nolan on the mound on August 4. I never, ever wanted to miss one of Nolan's starts. Those were always special games for me.

I wasn't shocked when Robin charged the mound in the top of the third inning. I knew that was going to happen the instant Nolan hit him with the pitch. There were a couple of things that happened during our previous series in Chicago, so that's what led to the fight that night in Arlington. Nolan threw it at him—I'm not saying otherwise—but it was just waiting to happen between the two teams. If you look at the video, I was already wrapped around Robin halfway, trying to hold him, when Nolan came forward. I remember Nolan coming down from the pitcher's mound and in front of the hill. That's when he grabbed Robin and started pounding him.

Usually when a pitcher intentionally hits a batter for payback, sending a message, that sort of stuff, he goes after the best hitter that you have in the lineup. Unfortunately, that poor guy is the one who is going to get hit. Robin Ventura was one of the best White Sox hitters at the time, and that's what happened. But that all depends on what happened in the game or the series before, things like that. There were some times I felt like I was hit on purpose, but I never charged the mound. I usually knew that I was going to get hit.

For example, I was playing against the Cleveland Indians one time and slid hard into perennial Gold Glove shortstop Omar Vizquel. And I injured him, knocking him out of the lineup for 15 days. That was in Texas, and the next time we went to Cleveland, Jose Mesa came in as a reliever and hit me right in the leg. I knew that was coming. So I picked the ball up and threw it back to Jose. I was looking at him, and he was looking at me and he didn't say anything.

The next day in batting practice, he came to me and shook my hand because I was very professional. It's part of the game. I didn't get mad with him because he hit me in the leg. It's a great spot to do that. I'm never a fan of hitting people, though sometimes it happens because there's a reason for it to happen. But I would never throw above the belt. That's so dangerous. I see some pitchers today who throw fastballs at 98 miles an hour right at the batter's head, and sometimes they don't realize how dangerous that is. You can kill somebody. Dickie Thon got hit in the eye and almost never played again. Everyone has seen the photo of Tony Conigliaro from 1967. Both could hardly see anything in the aftermath of being hit.

There's a lot that goes into it when a guy is thrown at intentionally. When things happened on the field that made us mad, we would talk about it. It's all about the situation, what's happening in the game, whether the game is close or it's a blowout. If the game is tied or it's late, we don't do things like that. It's just about picking a spot and a perfect situation to do it. But if it's not today, we'll keep it in our minds and take care of it later on.

Baseball players have long memories.

6

Behind the Plate

THERE WAS MUCH TO BE EXCITED ABOUT ENTERING THE 1994 campaign. We had signed Will Clark, an All-Star first baseman with one of the sweetest swings anyone has ever seen, that offseason, and few teams could match our offensive power with Juan Gonzalez, Dean Palmer, and Jose Canseco.

Also, the Rangers were moving into a new home. The Ballpark in Arlington, a magnificent jewel of a stadium, was one of my favorites in baseball. When an investment group headed by George W. Bush, who later became the 43rd president of the United States, bought the team in 1989, among the highest objectives was building a new, more modern stadium. And they hit a home run with The Ballpark, which had a capacity of a little more than 48,000. From what I've been told, there's not a bad seat in the house either.

Our former home was Arlington Stadium, which used to be a Triple A ballpark with a capacity of roughly 43,000. That was after multiple expansions. When it was built in 1965, it was originally called Turnpike Stadium and held 10,000. Then they just built the upper deck and put bleachers in once the Washington Senators announced they were moving there in 1971.

For me, it was fine obviously, especially compared to the minor league parks I played in coming up or even those in Puerto Rico. Heck, it was the big leagues. I would have been thrilled playing in a parking lot. But Arlington Stadium wasn't really considered all that nice. The clubhouse was very small, and everything was close together. And it was a long, dark tunnel from the clubhouse to the dugout. I do think the playing field was really good, though, almost perfect and so was the atmosphere. It was small obviously, and everything felt very intimate. It was built up by steel and iron to go from a 10,000-seat stadium to a 40,000-seat stadium. When you drove around it, you could see all the steel that was there to support the bleachers. I have great memories from there, and it was great ballpark for hitting.

The year before we moved into the new digs in 1993, a few of us went to the new ballpark and had batting practice there while it was still under construction. I remember it was me, Dean, Juan, and Rafael Palmeiro. It was cool, and we found out that the fly balls carried better, especially to the alley in right-center field. At least, they used to. Now they've put up these big panels and signs in center field, and those hold the breeze a little more. That ballpark is beautiful, but the new one, the one they just approved to build with the retractable roof, is going to be unbelievable. They're already working on it, and the first season is slated for 2020. Amazing how quickly they build ballparks nowadays. There's absolutely nothing wrong with what I knew as The Ballpark—now called Globe Life Park in Arlington. It's just that, well, it's really, really hot in the summer. I mean, really hot.

Of course, there's a big difference between playing in Arlington and playing on the road. Not just for the pitchers, but for everybody. Remember, when the pitchers are at home they can go inside really quick between innings. They pitch and then they go inside to the air conditioning. They can go straight to the clubhouse, refresh themselves, come back, and then pitch again. As for me, I would sometimes change my game jersey two or three times. The undershirt I would change every couple of innings. I drank a lot of water and Pedialyte and I would lose four to five pounds every game during the summer—sometimes more.

In Puerto Rico it's rare that the temperature touches 100 degrees. The problem there is that it's 92 or 95 but very muggy, humid, and sticky. In Texas it's both. As a player, though, I would have preferred to play in 100 degrees rather than 20 degrees. I was miserable playing in cold weather. If you look at some of the numbers early in the year when I was with Detroit, they weren't good. It was a different experience. When you play in the cold weather, you have a hard time getting loose and you feel the vibration of the bat more. It's tough to stay focused when your hands are freezing and you get jammed. Your hands go numb.

The heat is totally the opposite. I prefer to sweat. To me that's better, and trust me, I was having better at-bats later in the game. Like my third or fourth time up, when I had already lost a couple pounds, that's when I was having my best at-bats. If I didn't go through my training program during the offseason, maybe I wouldn't have played as well in September. But during my career, I was very good in August and September. When everybody was tired the last two months of the season, I was ready to go.

One of the highlights of my career took place in 1994 on July 28, when Kenny Rogers threw a perfect game in front of a sold-out home crowd. That was a magical night, and it was just the 12th perfect game thrown since 1900. It came against a pretty solid California Angels lineup, too, that featured the likes of Jim Edmonds, Chili Davis, Bo Jackson, and J.T. Snow.

Kenny came up a few years before me and was mostly a reliever during his first four seasons, making the occasional spot start. He became a full-time starter in 1993 and really had a fantastic career, winning 219 games. We were teammates again with the Detroit Tigers.

He was a control pitcher who could really hit his spots, though not when he was younger. Kenny was throwing in the middle 90s when he came up. So, he still had a good fastball to go along with all these good change-ups, a big curve, slider and he loved to throw the sinker. Later in his career, his sinker was like 81 or 82 miles per hour. When I caught him earlier, he was around 92 or 93 with the sinker, but he always loved to throw that pitch. He was a very competitive person—what I like to call a gamer— you could always depend on him come gameday. And he wanted everybody behind him to play hard for him. He expected the same commitment to winning as he was giving himself. For the most part, we always got along, had a solid working relationship, and there was definitely a mutual respect. Of course, like with any pitcher, we had our differences along the way.

KENNY ROGERS
RANGERS PITCHER

"I remember an interaction with me and him in Toronto in 1993. I had been around a while at this point and I knew what I was capable of doing. And Pudge had been around three years now himself.

"I know Pudge. He's got guys on base and he wants to throw some guys out. He popped down that one for the fastball, and I shook. Well, he popped it down again. And I shook. Well, I shook seven times because he kept putting one down. I knew what I wanted to do. I stepped off the mound in between, and then he put it down again and I shook. And he gave in and gave me the change-up that I wanted, and we got the guy out.

> "From that point on, I think he respected that. I think he just had to know that a pitcher is thinking along with the gameplan, too. We had a really good relationship, understanding what each other was capable of. That was just his way of finding out that I really did have the confidence in what I wanted to do."

Yeah, I remember that too. I gave Kenny the sign that I wanted a few times, and he said, "No, no, no." And then I went through all the pitches that he throws, and he said, "No, no, no." And I went like, "What do you want to throw?" And then he stepped up, and I went out to talk to him. And he said, "I want this pitch." I said, "Okay, I gave you that pitch twice already." But he said location was the issue.

After catching his perfect game in 1994, I told the media, "I feel like I went 4-for-4." There's nothing better than catching a perfect game. It was probably in the sixth or seventh inning that I realized from the fans there was a no-hitter going on. But after that we just had the same gameplan. There were some great plays that happened. You know Rusty Greer made some tremendous grabs for Kenny and made a couple diving catches, including one in the ninth inning to rob Rex Hudler. Then Gary DiSarcina hit a line drive to Greer that he caught for the last out. It was a great game. I'm sure everyone realizes this, but a lot of things have to go right for a perfect game to happen. You get great plays and get timely hitting, and then pitches that are probably balls are called strikes. A lot of things happen that go your way, which is why they so seldom occur.

When Kenny threw that perfect game, I caught him in the bullpen. And nothing in the bullpen was working. Fastballs, sliders, curveballs—he couldn't throw any of them well. Also, the change-up was too hard. And when we walked to the dugout, he told me, "I don't know what's going to happen today, but I don't think it's going to be a good day." Nothing worked for him in the bullpen, and look what happened. He started pitching great from the first pitch. Everything was working. The curve was perfect. The change-up was perfect. The sinker was perfect. The fastballs were up and in; four-seam fastballs were perfect. There was no pitch he threw that night that was out of location. Every pitch he threw was right there.

ROGERS

"He ignored me on the bench as the game went on, like your teammates do during a no-hitter or perfect game, but during the game when we were on the field, we had a good back-and-forth going. I didn't have to shake him off much at all. That game, it didn't matter what he put down. I felt great with everything. He was putting the signs down, and we were in a rhythm. That makes all the difference. Those rare times you are completely in rhythm with a catcher, you gain so much confidence in him, and he gains it in you. That is what you're looking for, being of the same mind.

"There's a relationship with the catcher that if it's off at all, those games don't happen. That mesh we had that night, that's how you get fortunate to do something like that."

We won the game 4–0. It barely took two hours because when one team doesn't put a guy on base the games tend to go pretty quickly. Canseco hit two solo home runs, and I hit one. The fans were pretty loud that night, and it was as much fun as any regular-season game of my career. To me, that's what being a catcher is all about, too. Calling a great game and helping a guy be at his very best, having a part in him accomplishing something only a few others ever have. Those are the games and moments you remember.

Less than two weeks after that electrifying night, our season ended. We didn't know it at the time, but our 3–2 loss against the Seattle Mariners on August 10 would be our last big league regular-season game for almost nine months. I finished my 1994 season batting .298 with 16 home runs and 57 RBIs in just 99 games. That was a 25-point jump at the plate, and I also won my first Silver Slugger award, meaning I was the top offensive catcher in the American League. That was pretty cool, considering a lot of folks thought I would be a defensive specialist when I came up. Sadly, for the first time in more than 90 years, there was no World Series. It would take the game years to rebound from that players' strike.

That was really difficult, but at the same time, that's part of baseball. That's why the MLB Players Association is one of the best in the industry. I'm very pleased with what they've done for the players and the way they protect us. The way the contracts are done today, they are fully guaranteed contracts, which is wonderful and ideal. Just think about it: you have an NFL player who has a five or six-year contract, and if he gets hit and can't play anymore, he's not getting paid. That's really dumb. That's not a good thing. And baseball is totally the opposite. If you get called up, hit the baseball for a few years, and sign a guaranteed multi-year contract, that's your money, no matter what happens going forward. If you're a pitcher and throw your arm out, that money is still there. From my perspective, that's fantastic because that's what you work for. You obviously work to be a great baseball player, but you also want to establish a future for your family. As an athlete, your primary earning years are much different than say an accountant or police officer, who is more than likely going to be making more money as they grow older into their 40s and 50s. We need to make the money when we can, when we are young and healthy.

When the strike happened, there were real issues that needed to be worked out. Looking back, I wish we would have found a way to work them out without doing that to the fans, but that's what it took. And it took almost a year to do it, but baseball finally came back. It took a little longer for the fans to come back to the game of baseball. They were mad and they didn't come out to the games. When we came back after the strike, attendance was probably 10,000 maximum. So, it was hard at the beginning, but thankfully the fans came back because it's the national pastime. Baseball in the summertime is baseball in the summertime. There are no other major sports going on, just baseball.

During the strike basically what I did was focus on training and keeping myself in shape. We had to keep ourselves in condition because they told us that if everything was resolved, we would have to come back and continue the baseball season. But it didn't happen. The end of September 1994 came and passed. Baseball was over. They cancelled everything.

What I did that year was I went to play winter ball for the entire season. That was one of the best years there because *everybody* was playing winter ball. I mean all the big leaguers were playing. That was a great, very competitive season. All six teams had three or four major leaguers, and we were drawing great crowds, too. That was the only baseball you could see because there was no more big league baseball.

Fortunately for the big league game, during that September after we returned in 1995, Cal Ripken Jr. broke Lou Gehrig's streak for most consecutive games played. That was a special moment, and Ripken couldn't have handled himself any better, running around the field and high-fiving the fans. No one signed more autographs than Cal, and that helped with a lot of baseball fans around the country.

When we returned in late April 1995 after an abbreviated spring training, the Rangers did so with new leadership: Doug Melvin was the new general manager, and Johnny Oates was our new manager.

A lot of people, ourselves included, felt like we were ready to compete for a division title at that point. The pitching wasn't quite there to balance our potent lineup, though Kenny really had come into his own as one of the league's elite left-handed starters. We finished in third place, four games over .500. I batted .300 for the first time and hit two of my 12 homers that season off Roger Clemens at Fenway Park on July 13. We won that game 9–8. That was the first multi-homer game of my career, and to do it against the only man to win seven Cy Young awards made it all the better. Clemens pitched a lot like Nolan did. He was not afraid to come inside. He was intimidating on the mound and more or less impossible to hit many nights.

That following season, it finally came together for us. We won the first division title in franchise history. We did something that can never, ever be replicated. We were the first, and that was an incredible feeling. We won 90 games. And our lineup was pretty stacked. Heck, our shortstop, Kevin Elster, hit 24 home runs and collected 99 RBIs hitting ninth all season. We finished fourth in the American League in runs scored and home runs with 928 and 221, respectively.

We felt in spring training that we had a good team, but I think we started to feel it more after the All-Star break. Everything started to get going the way we wanted it to. And the key was how much we bonded as a team then, how the chemistry and unity brought that group of people all together. It helped that most of us were playing some of the best baseball of our careers. We wanted to keep that. We didn't want everybody to split off this way and that way. When that happens to a team, the chemistry can fall apart. So the good thing was that a lot of us stayed there as a team, as a unit, as a group. I think that helped us to get where we wanted to be.

You have to get along with your teammates in order to play well because you'll be seeing each other's faces for at least six months—plus spring training and the playoffs. And the families, the wives, and kids have to get along. They're in the stands together on the road and at home. Everything has to come together. And it did for us in 1996, which would be the first of three division titles in four years.

Obviously, the unfortunate news was that when we won, we had to face the New York Yankees in the playoffs each of those seasons. And when we played them, it was like we had no chance. George Steinbrenner was spending money like crazy, bringing the best players in the game to the Yankees, and they were dominant, one of the great dynasties in the history of the sport. We peaked at the wrong time in baseball history. A lot of that is luck, too, like anything else. It's timing.

I was able to play in a career-high 153 games during that 1996 season and I went to the plate nearly 700 times. I batted .300, reached career highs with 19 home runs and 86 RBIs, and scored 116 runs, which tied Yogi Berra for most runs scored by a catcher in a season. I also set a major league record for catchers with 47 doubles.

Juan, though, went absolutely nuts. Despite missing 28 games, he hit 47 home runs and finished with 144 RBIs. He had

10 more RBIs than games played, which is unheard of. He was named American League MVP, which was really cool for me to have a guy from my hometown being crowned as the best in the game. It's crazy to think about: Juan and I are from the same town, which had a population around 50,000 when we were growing up. What are the odds of us even making the big leagues—never mind that we both won MVP awards?

Much has been written and said about the relationship between us. We played in Little League against one another, though never on the same team. And then when he became a professional, he signed two years before I signed. Juan is the same age as my brother—two years older than I. We would see each other when we played in Little League. He went to the same school that I did and he was always around.

Fast forward to professional baseball, he was already in Double A when I signed, and then the Rangers called him up. In the big leagues, we didn't really go out together too much. He had his family; I had mine. He did his thing; I did mine. We would always see each other at the ballpark. On the road sometimes we would go to dinner but not all the time. The relationship was very good with him. Right now I think we are very good friends, though I don't have many conversations with him because he never picks up the phone. But when we see each other, we get along very well.

We were close, but what I'm saying is that it was not 24 hours a day of being together. Outside of the ballpark, we would see each other every once in a while. My ex-wife and his first wife got along well, so sometimes we would go to their home or they would come to ours. He was my closest teammate there for a good stretch, but we weren't joined at the hip like some made it out to be.

He was a good teammate, but sometimes he would get mad, and nobody could talk to him. He would just disappear, just go somewhere or leave the clubhouse, and nobody would see him. The manager and the coaches needed to be smart about how to talk to him. He would get mad quickly, though not mad at everybody else, just himself. When he didn't like something, he just shut down. But when he came ready to play baseball, he was the best. He has to be considered one of the great power hitters of his time.

Looking back, I guess Juan and I were just different in how we approached things—from the media to learning English to taking part in charity work. That doesn't make it right or wrong. I just feel like at times—because we were from the same town and whatnot—that we were lumped in as Juan and Pudge, not as individuals.

JOHN BLAKE
RANGERS EXECUTIVE VICE PRESIDENT OF COMMUNICATIONS

"Juan and Pudge came up around the same time, especially in terms of when they started getting a lot of national attention. We needed to work with them more and we were the first team to bring someone in to work with our Hispanic players, that being Luis Mayoral. Juan was very shy in terms of talking to the media. Juan was much tougher, but Pudge became pretty good as the years went on.

"Pudge always had an infectious smile. Early on he wanted to become more involved in the community. He did a ton of charity work and clinics. He was different than Juan, who was much more withdrawn, much tougher to work with.

"When Pudge won the 1999 MVP he was at Disney World, and we didn't even think he was going to win it. It was kind of a surprise. Pedro Martinez was the prohibitive favorite. So, Pudge was on vacation at Disney World, but he flew back that night to do the press conference. And Juan wouldn't have done that in a hundred years. Juan won two MVPs, and he wasn't here for either one of them. He was in Puerto Rico.

"Pudge really became pretty good on multiple fronts— the community and the media. He really did a nice job, and that's one of the reasons he's so beloved by the fans to this day."

Know what is sometimes forgotten about those three postseason series against the Yankees? Yes, we lost nine straight playoff games to them, but we didn't lose that first one. That was the adrenalin rush of a lifetime. We beat New York 6–2 at Yankee Stadium on October 1, 1996, in front of more than 57,000 fans. That place was electric. Juan hit a three-run homer off David Cone in the fourth inning, and John Burkett went the distance for us. I probably remember as much about that game as any I ever played in. The environment was just so different than the regular season. Nothing replicates postseason baseball.

7

The MVP

My brother, Tito, and I get ready for our first season of Little League in Puerto Rico. *(Ivan Rodriguez Family)*

On the baseball field and off, Tito and I were constant companions. *(Ivan Rodriguez Family)*

I play on the national championship team in Puerto Rico for the six- to nine-year-old category. *(Ivan Rodriguez Family)*

From my earliest days, I was groomed to be a backstop. *(Ivan Rodriguez Family)*

Always a passionate baseball player, I await another season of Little League. *(Ivan Rodriguez Family)*

I go through my first communion in Vega Baja, Puerto Rico, along with my brother, Tito. *(Ivan Rodriguez Family)*

Tito and I hang with my grandfather, Chago. *(Ivan Rodriguez Family)*

Tito and I hang with my grandparents, Funfa and Chago. *(Ivan Rodriguez Family)*

Always a competitor, I have my game face on while playing with my Puerto Rican team, the Raiders. *(Ivan Rodriguez Family)*

In the blue T-shirt, I hang out with my Raiders teammates, including my brother, Tito, who is in the white undershirt. *(Ivan Rodriguez Family)*

I play on the Tulsa Drillers, which served as the Texas Rangers' Double A affiliate from 1977 to 2002. *(Ivan Rodriguez Family)*

I hold my son, Dereck, during his baptism in Puerto Rico. The Minnesota Twins later drafted him in the sixth round of the 2011 draft. *(Ivan Rodriguez Family)*

The mayor of my hometown of Vega Baja, Puerto Rico, honors me. *(Ivan Rodriguez Family)*

I love hanging out with my family. From left to right, my Uncle Julio, Uncle Santiago, me, and my father pose for a picture. (*Ivan Rodriguez Family*)

Joined by my mom, Eva, and wife, Patricia Gomez, in San Francisco, I enjoy my final and 14th All-Star Game in 2007. (*Ivan Rodriguez Family*)

Throughout my 21-year major league career, including five seasons with the Tigers, my mom was my No. 1 fan. (*Ivan Rodriguez Family*)

I had the pleasure of visiting the second graders at my mother's school in Puerto Rico. *(Ivan Rodriguez Family)*

I am close to my family, including my little brother, Manuelito, and my father, Jose. *(Ivan Rodriguez Family)*

My Uncle Julio and I hug my grandma, who we always called Funfa. *(Ivan Rodriguez Family)*

AT VARIOUS TIMES OF MY CAREER—FROM WHEN SCOUTS WERE clocking me in Puerto Rico to the minor leagues to the Rangers—I was clocked throwing from home to second base in anywhere from 1.70 to 1.80 seconds. Two full seconds is considered solid, and anything in the 1.90s is really quick, top-tier. That's from glove to glove, what we call "pop time," not from the moment the ball leaves my hand.

There weren't a lot of guys running on me, as word spread pretty quickly from the time I came up. When they did run on me, it usually ended poorly on their end. I led the American League in caught-stealing percentage nine times overall, including six straight years from 1996 to 2001. Over that stretch I threw out 55 percent of would-be base stealers. The remainder of the catchers in the American League over that same six-year run threw out less than 30 percent. For my career I ended up throwing out nearly 45.7 percent. In the last 40 years, the great Yadier Molina is second, and he was at 41.7 percent entering the 2017 season.

I also picked off 88 runners in my career, which is a major league record for catchers. I don't think anyone keeps track of how many times I threw down to a base in an attempt to pick someone off, but here's betting that's easily a record number as well. Make no mistake, I was aggressive.

Yes, I am also well aware that some pitchers thought I called for too many fastballs, especially early in my career with runners on base, since it would be easier for me to throw them out. Every pitch I called in my life was with the best intention of helping my team. If I thought a runner was going to steal, then yeah, maybe I would have called for a fastball because that was better for throwing him out. To be honest, though, not a lot of guys were stealing on me in the first place. In the prime of my career, opposing teams were attempting to steal less than once every two games. Thus, it would be ridiculous for me to call fastballs every time someone was on base.

There would be some occasions when I knew the base stealer was out before the ball left my hand, maybe even before that. First off, it all depends on how much the pitcher helps me. If the pitcher has a slow delivery to home plate, it's going to be hard for me. It doesn't matter how strong of an arm I have; there's no chance. There is no way. But I can tell you that when it's a decent delivery to the plate, say 1.3 seconds, maybe even 1.4, I know that the runner is going to be out. I enjoyed my defense more than hitting. That doesn't include just throwing. It means calling a great game, blocking balls, and making sure the pitcher feels comfortable with me behind the plate.

The way that I would decide when to try a pickoff was by reaction. It was by instinct. I also anticipated obviously and I had to communicate with the position player who would take the throw. He needed to look at me all the time. It's a signal that I always put on. Some of the signals I put on were obvious, but the plays never happened. And some of them were so good that very few could notice them. But every time there were runners on base, everyone—first, second, short, third—had to look at me all the time. All the time.

A lot of the play happens when the pitcher is going into his motion. After I gave the sign, you'd have to look at me because I might put on a different sign. That way I could decoy the other bench—even the managers and the coaches. When the pitcher is in his motion, everyone is looking at the baseball leaving the hand. And that was a good time for me to give a sign. The runner wasn't looking at me, and neither were the coaches at first and third base.

I picked off a lot of guys with two outs. And I would love it if catchers did that more in baseball, but nobody pays attention to it. With two outs the runners are thinking, *I've got to get a bigger lead because I've got to score.* Especially when the best hitter in the lineup is up, that's when it's the best time to do it. If there are two outs and the cleanup batter is at the plate, I want to clear the bases. I want this guy to lead off the next inning because then if he hits a home run it's only one run instead of two or three.

Although pitchers and coaches here and there asked me about my aggressive pitch calling with runners on base, no one was too upset about it, as I am pretty sure everyone was happy with the all-around package I was bringing to the catcher position. But one guy who got on me—and I mean got in my face about pitch calling and even some of my aggressive pickoff attempts—was Will Clark. Or "The Thrill," as he was often called going back to his days with the San Francisco Giants. This guy could flat-out hit. In the 1989 National League Championship Series, he batted .650 against the Chicago Cubs.

Those first few seasons he was with the Rangers in 1994–95, there were many times he aggressively approached me before, during, and after games. Not so much confrontationally, but that was just how Will was.

WILL CLARK
RANGERS FIRST BASEMAN

"We had some arguments, that's for sure. I took my role as a veteran serious, and even though he came up early, I was eight years older than him and by 1995 I was in my 10th big league season. When I thought he was calling fastballs for the wrong reason, I'd tell him and explain why it was the wrong call. Not only for his pitcher but the defense. And Pudge didn't like people telling him he was wrong.

"There were times he was throwing the ball down to first base when I was playing behind the runner. One of the great advantages we had was that because of his arm no one was taking a lead at first. I called it the 'Drop Anchor Effect.' Guys get to first, drop anchor. So why would I leave my spot so he could whip the ball down there with a guy half a foot off the bag.

"Thing is, we started talking more and more and pretty soon we're sitting together on the back of every flight talking baseball. We were baseball nerds. We would break down the pitching staff for the next series, go over the game we just played, not batter-by-batter, but pitch-by-pitch. Pudge ended up being one of my all-time favorite teammates, and I've never seen a better catcher in my life."

It was a little bumpy sometimes because Will is Will. I always came to the park and wanted to do a good job. And don't get me wrong, when I was a player, there were times I would get mad. That's probably why he just told me to calm down and chill out. But Will was a world-class teammate. He was a guy who always came ready to do his job. He was always serious and never laughed when he played. Once the game was over, though, he was a different person in the clubhouse, a guy who played around and cared about the other players. He was the kind of guy who would come in and tell you when you weren't playing hard. He would say, "Let's go, step up, and play hard."

We became good friends and we started to respect each other. After maybe a year, he realized the type of everyday player I was. That's probably why he started to become a good friend of mine. He saw that I was playing every day behind the plate, not taking a day off, and I think that's one of the things that he liked about me.

One of the things I really didn't like as a player was when another fielder thought they knew the best pitches to call. I knew that we were all teammates and we were all there to win a ballgame. But I really didn't like seeing a teammate in the playing field react to the pitch I called, especially if it was hit hard or went for a home run. I would see somebody get mad, and that's one thing I could not stand. I'm guessing that Will did some of that, and we started talking seriously at that time. During such a conversation, I would tell him, "You do your job, and I'll do mine." I took a lot of pride in what I did, going and studying, trying to get the best information possible. It made me mad when I was in the video room, making all these notes, and they were all in the batting cages hitting baseballs.

Will didn't do it again after we talked, and we became great teammates and lifelong friends. It was a good thing for me and for everybody. That's one of the good qualities I have as a person—I try not to judge anyone. The guy who you think is the biggest asshole at first might turn out to be a good friend. That's the person that I am. I tried to be friends with everybody.

The 1997 season was disappointing for us to say the least. We were coming off a division crown and we finished 77–85, third in the American League West. We had a lot of injuries that year. Will and Juan Gonzalez missed nearly 100 games between them. We also traded our third baseman, Dean Palmer, in July for speedy center fielder Tom Goodwin. That one didn't make much sense to me. Palmer had without question the quickest swing I've ever seen. That guy could turn on a pitch in an instant and many times take one deep. From 1998 to 2000, he hit 101 home runs, and we definitely could have used that production. Dean didn't always receive the credit he deserved, but he was just an outstanding all-around ballplayer.

One of the more remarkable days of my career came that season on July 31, which each and every year is also the trading deadline. My agent at the time, Jeffrey Moorad, had been negotiating a contract extension for more than a year and wasn't having much success. That was the last year of my deal. I was making $6.65 million and I wanted to stay in Texas. I didn't want to be a free agent. The team's general manager, Doug Melvin, was handling the negotiations and said publically during spring training that catchers decline in their performance after 900 big league games. I started that year at 730, so he was reluctant to sign me to a long-term deal. He said, "It's nothing against Pudge. Catcher is just a high-risk, wear-and-tear position."

Two days before the deadline, the Rangers traded starting pitcher Ken Hill to the Anaheim Angels for catcher Jim Leyritz, which to me meant they were planning to deal me rather than offer the extension we were looking for. I was really stressed out. I didn't want to leave. We flew home from Baltimore on July 30 and had the following day off. I was sitting with Juan on the flight, and he was begging me to talk with team president Tom Schieffer. I later found out that I was about to be traded to the New York Yankees for catcher Jorge Posada and pitcher Tony Armas Jr.

The next morning I called my mother, and she agreed with Juan: it was time to take control of the situation myself. My wife also agreed. At 9:00 AM there I was at Schieffer's office at the stadium. Just me, no agent. I told him point-blank; there was no small talk, none of that. I just said, "I don't want to be traded. I want to stay here. I want to wear this Rangers uniform my entire career."

He told me to sit down, and we quickly negotiated a five-year, $42 million contract and shook hands. That doesn't happen enough, and what I did certainly didn't start a trend. How often do we all hear athletes say in retrospect that they wish they had stayed with the team they used to be with? Plus, it's not like I was playing for minimum wage, you know, I was guaranteed to be paid $42 million. I was going to be able to take care of my family—present and future. There's also something to be said for staying where you are happy.

A few weeks after that, I appeared on the cover of *Sports Illustrated*. That was a pretty big deal since I was just the fourth Ranger at the time to be on the cover, joining manager Billy Martin, infielder Bump Wills, and the immortal Nolan Ryan. That was a great honor. Looking back at the story, there are two quotes that kind of stand out.

From my ex-wife Maribel: "Ivan doesn't drink or smoke. He doesn't go out. His only bad habit, if you want to call it that, is that he watches ESPN when he comes home from the ballpark at night. Then he gets up in the morning, takes a shower, and watches ESPN again. Honestly, I don't get it."

She was right about that. Especially during the baseball season, I was a pretty boring guy. I lived baseball. There was a little time for family, but otherwise, it was 24/7 baseball. When I would be watching other baseball games, or watching the highlights on ESPN, I was always focused on the teams we would be playing soon. I was always, always, always making mental notes about the situation when I was watching the games, always seeing what the leadoff guy does, how many pitches he takes, what pitch he wants to see so he can put the ball in play. I was always looking at how many times the second batter hit the ball the other way or how often he hit the ball in the hole between first and second when the leadoff guy got on base. I wanted to see what pitches the third, fourth, and fifth-place hitters were looking for—both with nobody on and with men in scoring position. Don't get me wrong; I wasn't watching every single game. Normally the games that I watched involved the teams I was going to play against next. If I was at home and Seattle was coming to town next, I was watching the Mariners series. If Anaheim was coming to town in a month, I would watch the Angels games and write a few things down. Especially when they were out on the West Coast because then I had time to come home and watch them.

I usually just remembered that stuff. My memory is one of the best qualities that I have. Not just in baseball, but in everyday life. Ask anyone who knows me. I can drive a car to an address somewhere and I won't need an address if I go back there again. I remember how to get there.

The second thing from that *SI* article is from Johnny Oates, my manager who I adored and respected so much. I just had the utmost admiration for him. No one managed me longer either. From 1995 to 2001, he was my skipper for nearly 1,000 games. Tragically, he was diagnosed with a brain tumor and passed away in 2004 at just 58 years old. In the story Johnny said, "If he stays healthy, I guarantee he'll be making an acceptance speech someday. In my 30 years in baseball, the closest total package I've seen to Pudge is Johnny Bench."

That meant a lot to me because Bench was my idol. I was just 25 years old at the time, but Johnny Oates was such a smart baseball man. I just wish he could've been there in Cooperstown to see me on stage.

In 1998 we won another AL West crown, finishing 88–74 and edging the Angels by three games. We finished second in the league in runs scored, and I set career highs across the board, batting .321 with 21 home runs and 91 RBIs. I also collected my 100th career home run and 1,000th career hit. Juan won another MVP award with a ridiculous 157 RBIs.

However, the Yankees won 114 games, which was the most since 1906. Again, just bad timing on our part in terms of baseball history. They were our first-round opponents, and we scored one run in three games. It's tough to win when you're scoring a run in three games.

The following year was the best Rangers team I played on, and we went 95–67. We had a lot of guys put up big numbers. Rafael Palmeiro batted .324 with 47 home runs and 148 RBIs, Juan hit .326 with 39 home runs and 128 RBIs, Rusty Greer batted .300 and drove in 101 runs, Todd Zeile and Lee Stevens each hit 24 home runs, and Mark McLemore scored 105 runs. We were an offensive juggernaut. The pitching was solid, too, with Aaron Sele winning 18 games and John Wetteland saving 43.

My season started hot and remained that way throughout. On April 13 at Seattle, I had nine RBIs through four innings against the Mariners. I hit a three-run homer in the first, a two-run single in the second, and my first career grand slam in the fourth.

That was as much fun as I ever had coming to the ballpark every day. We were winning, which is always nice, and I was seeing the ball so well at the plate. I ended up batting .332 with 35 home runs and 113 RBIs. I also scored 116 runs and stole 25 bases. It was the first time a catcher ever hit 20 home runs and stole 20 bases in the same season, which I was proud of. In an extremely close vote—with Pedro Martinez finishing second—I was voted the American League MVP. It didn't make up for another postseason sweep by the Yankees, which was becoming really old and frustrating. But the MVP award is what every player dreams about. I was immensely proud of that accomplishment. We had taken the family to Disney World for the first time and we just arrived the night before the vote was announced. I wasn't expecting to win, but they called, and we took the next flight to Arlington for the press conference. Then we went back to Disney World.

All that was a result of hard work. It's not easy to get there. The only thing you can control is working hard, making sure that when you're in there, playing nine innings, 27 outs for three and a half hours, you do the best that you can. When you do those things, you're going to start winning awards. And that's the way I always did it.

I was taught to play with pain growing up. That's the main thing you have to do as a catcher. It's rare that you are playing at 100 percent. I'd be out there on any given day with pain in my lower back, legs, hands, and arms. When we would be stretching, we'd focus on the soreness. No matter what, though, I worked out every morning—both in the offseason and during the year. That was my fix, and I needed that to keep going. It became a routine. Staying healthy, eating right, working out, all of that becomes a whole lot easier when it's routine.

A Major League Baseball season is 162 games, and from spring training until the postseason, that's nine months at the highest intensity. As an athlete let's say in the NBA or NHL, that's 82 games. A football season is 16 games. In baseball we have to be at our highest level almost every day for those six months of the regular season, running the bases hard, throwing as hard as you can on every stolen base attempt or pickoff, swinging hard, using your agility to move right and left of the plate to block pitches. That's what you're doing for three or four hours a night, and when that's the case, anyone is going to wake up the next morning feeling pain.

It's not natural to be squatting down like that. There's a reason you don't see people squatting during normal walks of life because it's not comfortable. Then factor in blocking balls in the dirt, not to mention the fact that I'm throwing the ball back to the pitcher the entire time. There are no relief catchers for when my arm is tired or sore. There are no pitch counts for catchers.

If you include the bullpen sessions, I'm guessing I threw 200 pitches a day, every day. So my arm needed to be strong enough to endure that. And I was usually throwing the ball back to the pitcher at a decent clip. Some people were curious why I had my own personal trainer. It's because I needed to be physically ready for those challenges during the season.

Thank God my arm doesn't have any scars. Even with throwing that much and pitching into my teens, I never really had any elbow soreness. It's incredible to think about how fortunate I was. I'm sure it helped that I did a lot of stretching on my own, with my personal trainer, and with the team. As for ice you always see pitchers icing their arms after games. Like most of us from Puerto Rico, I hate the cold. And I never liked how the ice felt on my arm, so—outside of a few times when a trainer was really pushing me—I never used ice.

I was blessed with a great arm, a young arm, and my arm always stayed young. I can still throw it with a little pop. I would bet Nolan and I can still throw it faster than some guys in the big leagues. Nolan is much older than I am, but I'd take that bet.

One thing we focused on with the stretching and the weights was my rotator cuff, which holds the muscles and tendons that surround the shoulder joint and is obviously instrumental to throwing. It's important to stress that we are talking about small ligaments and small tendons around your elbow and shoulder, so when we were lifting weights to focus on these areas, it was three and five-pound dumbbells. I was never looking to bulk up there—just keep it flexible and solid.

I was lucky with injuries. I played in 2,543 games, which entering the 2017 season was tied for 47th in Major League Baseball history. In the prime of my career, from 1992 to 2007, I played in 82 percent of my team's games. For a catcher that's something I take a lot of pride in. My goal was to play 150 games each season, and, while that only happened a few times, setting the standard high made me push myself to be on the field each and every day. That's the No. 1 objective for any athlete, really more than hitting home runs or scoring touchdowns. It's just being out there.

That's without question what I am most impressed with when looking back. I was able to take the field so often, playing 21 seasons in the big leagues and catching until the very end. That final season with the Washington Nationals I caught 37 games and played first base just once. The individual awards like Gold Gloves were nice, but what I hope my teammates and coaches remember is that I was able to play as much as I did.

There were a few stints on the disabled list. A herniated disk in 2002, my final year with the Rangers, limited me to 108 games. I hurt my knee one year playing winter ball in Puerto Rico. There were an assortment of minor injuries later in my career. The big one came in 2000, though, when I suffered a season-ending injury. I broke my thumb when I hit Mo Vaughn's bat on a throw down to second base. That was on July 24 against Anaheim. I underwent surgery the following day, and they inserted four pins. Mo definitely didn't mean to hit me. It was completely accidental. He even said after the game, "It's just unfortunate because he's such a great player. Something will be missed from the game these last two months."

That was brutal, not being able to play the final two months of the season. I knew it was broken immediately. I didn't even look at it. I was just holding my hand until the trainer came out. When we walked off the field, I looked and saw the bone hanging out. It was disgusting.

Know what, though, that wasn't in my control. Breaking my thumb was tough, but I needed to have a strong mentality and try to be as positive as I could be. When I was around the team in the locker room, I was extremely positive. It happened, and I can't control or change it.

No one ever talks about Pudge the hitter. It's always Pudge the catcher. And that's fine. I took a lot of pride in my defense. I want people to think of my defense first. Every time I threw out a runner or picked someone off the base paths, I enjoyed that so much. Honestly, I don't even talk about my hitting. However, during that 2000 season, I was seeing the ball really well. And my numbers were better than even my MVP season a year before.

I played in 91 of our 97 games at the time of the injury. If you average out what I was doing to 144 games, which was actually a more modest pace than I was on, my numbers would have included a .347 batting average, 44 home runs, 44 doubles, 135 RBI, and 206 hits. The only two players in baseball history to post those numbers in a single season are Babe Ruth in 1921 and Lou Gehrig in 1927. That would have been quite the list to join for sure. Offensively speaking, that season was definitely my peak. I was 28 years old.

I didn't change anything in terms of my catching style because of that injury. It was a fluky accident, which never happened to me before or after, so I couldn't worry about it. I just tried to be the best teammate I could be. I was at the ballpark for every home game in the dugout, offering support, cheering, doing whatever I could.

8

A-Rod and the Departure

AFTER MY ROOKIE SEASON, I REALLY BECAME A CREATURE OF habit during the baseball season, especially when we were at home. When you're on the road, it's a little more difficult, and that's not even factoring in travel days and three and four-hour flights. When we were playing in Arlington, though, my routine almost never changed.

I would wake up around 6:30 or 7:00, have a regular breakfast, drink some coffee. Even today, I'm a big coffee drinker. We would work out at 10:00 AM for an hour to 90 minutes, depending on if we did extra stretching. And even on the road, my personal trainer, Edgar Diaz, traveled with me for years. Then, if we were home, I'd go back and rest at the house, maybe take a nap, until leaving for the ballpark. I'd have lunch at the house, then head to the ballpark at 1:30.

Once at the park, I'd go over the scouting reports, watch some video, meet with that day's starting pitcher and the pitching coach. My goal was always giving the best information to our pitchers. I never spent time worrying about the pitcher we were facing. All my time and energy went toward preparing our staff and being ready for their lineup.

At that point it was time for stretching and then batting practice, maybe playing a little pepper. I always liked taking ground balls at third base, too. Then I'd meet again with that night's starting pitcher. That final hour before taking the field, there's usually some baseball on the TV. That would also be the only time that I could spend with family. Some guys have a bite to eat, but I couldn't digest the food that quickly, so I'd wait and eat after the game. There were many nights I wouldn't eat dinner until after midnight. Then I'd try and get at least six hours of sleep. That was my goal—to have at least six hours of sleep. Honestly, I'm not a very good sleeper. I could blame it on the adrenalin following games, but I really didn't sleep any better during the offseason or even now that I'm retired.

I don't like being alone either. I always liked having someone around to talk with, watch a game with. That's why Edgar traveled with me so much, and my brother would travel a lot or stay at the house if we were at home. My father would come visit a few times during the season. I was always trying to have someone around to avoid the loneliness.

Tito Rodriguez
Older Brother

"Even when he was younger, he never liked being alone. We were together almost every night until we fell asleep. Then when he was playing in the big leagues, he dreaded ever being alone. At times he had so many people with him that when he finally was tired, Ivan would have to sleep on the couch; the beds were all taken. There were many, many times the sun would be rising, and we're still there watching ESPN. He would sleep only for about two or three hours most nights on road trips. Road trips were the killers. He always slept more at home. Even today, he doesn't sleep too much because he's always watching the Golf Channel.

"He was always going through the scouting reports, too, asking everyone what happened in baseball today, how did this guy pitch, where's the box score. He'd stay up and watch the late games, he'd be taking notes, saying he needed to see the pitchers for later in the season. And you could see how sleepy he was, how exhausted he was, but he'd stay up. We would beg him to sleep, but he would always refuse. He needed more baseball."

The big news of the 2000–01 offseason was the Rangers' signing of Alex Rodriguez. The historic deal was for 10 years and $252 million, which truly shocked the baseball world. That was far and away the highest contract ever signed. And the thing is, by all accounts, no one else was offering anywhere close to what our owner, Tom Hicks, agreed to pay him.

At the time I was making $8.2 million and I was one season removed from winning league MVP. And I would have had a shot at another MVP if not for the season-ending thumb injury the year before. And now A-Rod was going to be making three times as much as I did. The biggest deal in sports history before that was basketball player Kevin Garnett signing for $126 million, which was half what Alex got. It was pretty crazy, mind-boggling to think about. The only bigger deals to this day, 16 years later, were A-Rod's extension ($275 million for 10 years) with the New York Yankees and Giancarlo Stanton's deal ($325 million for 13 years) with the Miami Marlins, which began in 2015.

Still, I heavily recruited him to play with the Rangers. I was talking to him almost every day for more than a month. Alex starting calling me Barry Switzer, the legendary college football coach at Oklahoma, because I was recruiting him so hard.

I thought with A-Rod that we had a shot at winning a World Series. Even a playoff series would have been nice since I was now entering my 10th season, and we had won exactly *one* playoff game. Instead, we finished last in the American League West in 2001, and Johnny Oates was fired after an 11–17 start. Jerry Narron, a very laid-back, very calm manager, replaced Johnny. Very quiet and really friendly, Narron was available for everything, any time, any place. If you wanted him to be at the ballpark at 1:00, he was there at 12:30. For anything that his players wanted to make them better, he was always available before the game, during the game, after the game; it didn't matter. I really wish we played better for him. Instead we finished last again the following season in 2002, and he was let go.

I don't think the clubhouse changed any when Alex Rodriguez came to Texas. The only thing I saw was that all the attention obviously went to the highest paid player. I didn't care about that. I was a player who came and did my best and gave advice to anyone who asked, which Alex did ask for. Everybody in the clubhouse did; it wasn't only Alex. I was a teammate of his for two years and I didn't have any problems with him. When he left I think the organization was going in a different direction. It wasn't because of what he did or didn't do. They just wanted to change things and obviously dump some of that contract. They weren't winning either. That didn't help.

Honestly, though, Alex never showed me a sense of entitlement or anything because if he had I would have stopped him for sure.

I didn't have problems with many teammates. The majority of the players that played with me loved me as a teammate, but there were some who didn't. Because I played the game to win and, if I saw somebody who wasn't hustling the way the rest of the team was, I'd go and talk to them. I like people who play the game hard, though I can't say that I played my hardest every single time. I was a lazy ass sometimes. But then I would punish myself. I would have other players come and tell me, "Hey, if you want us to play hard, do the same." I appreciated that. After the game I would go to the locker room, hug them, and say, "Thank you for telling me." I guess sometimes you take things for granted, and those are the things that you're not supposed to be doing as a ballplayer. And I did them sometimes—like not running out a ground ball. I'm a human like everybody else. If I was pushing my teammates to do it and I didn't do it, what kind of example would that set? So, I really tried to be aware of how I carried myself—both for my teammates and the kids watching me.

We played our 2001 season opener in Puerto Rico at Hiram Bithorn Stadium in San Juan. That was a special day, and we did clinics and worked with younger kids over the three days we spent there. It meant so much to the people there. Baseball plays such a significant role in the heritage there. It's really just as important as the food we eat. So, having a major league game there was a big deal. We lost the game 8–1, but the memories are more about working with the children and having all my family and friends around.

For the seventh straight season, I batted at least .300, finishing at .308 in 2001. For how we finished, losing 89 games, our offense was pretty potent. A-Rod hit 52 home runs and drove in 135, and Rafael Palmeiro wasn't far off with 47 and 123. The problem was the pitching; our 5.71 ERA was easily the highest in the league and the highest in franchise history. In fact, to this day, it's the third highest for any American League team since 1950.

My season ended early, as right knee soreness eventually was diagnosed as patella tendinitis. I was placed on the disabled list and underwent season-ending knee surgery on September 8. That was disappointing because I was really locked in at the plate, batting nearly .350 in July and August. Again, I always hit the ball better in the warm weather months, as I'm betting the majority of players from Puerto Rico and the Dominican Republic also do.

On September 11, 2001, I wasn't with my teammates in Oakland. I was at home in Carrolton, Texas, recovering from my surgery. I definitely think commissioner Bud Selig and the league did the right thing postponing games for a week. No one wanted to play baseball after such a tragic event.

Early in the 2002 season, I was diagnosed with a herniated disk in my lower back, which sidelined me for nearly two months. Not that there's ever a good time for an injury, but both team-wise and individually, this timing couldn't have been worse. Juan Gonzalez, who was back in Texas after a couple of seasons away; our No. 1 starter, Chan Ho Park; and our closer, Jeff Zimmerman were already on the disabled list, and it was also the last year of my contract. The organization had already made big-money deals with Park and outfielder Carl Everett—not to mention the A-Rod deal—and we still weren't winning, so I could kind of see the direction we were headed. It's a business, and there's only so much money to go around.

Still, I just wanted to play the best ball I could and see how it all ended up. I was also 30 years old, and when it came to catchers, many believed 30 was the new 40, meaning I was closer to being finished than having any more solid years in me. I wasn't helping myself prove that theory wrong either by missing 176 games because of various injuries those last three years with the Rangers.

When I was working my way back from the back injury, the Rangers came to me and asked about changing positions so my career would last longer. In retrospect, maybe they would have been more interested in signing me to an extension if I did agree. I don't know, I've never really thought about it until this very moment. Regardless, I said no. And it took me all of two seconds to say no. My father had me convinced from when I changed positions as a kid that I was truly born to catch.

I am pretty sure that he's been proven correct. I was born to catch.

What I would often do over my career is take some grounders at third base, my first position, along with pitcher, back in youth ball. Maybe I could have been a big league third baseman, but I don't know because I never tried to do it. I played some first base near the end of my career. That was probably because I've got good hands. I was so quick behind the plate that I probably could have been an okay third baseman, though I have never really thought about it. Then again, I was always bugging my managers to let me hit left-handed in a game, too. I used to hit some home runs during batting practice from the left side of the plate, but none of them would sign off. In an alternative life, I could have been a switch-hitting third baseman.

My first game back from the back injury was during an interleague series against the Atlanta Braves in early June. I went 4-for-4 and raised my batting average 64 points in that one game. From there I ended up having a pretty good year, batting .314 with 19 home runs.

After winning 10 straight Gold Gloves, which tied Johnny Bench for catchers, my run ended in 2002. I wasn't disappointed, though, because it was snapped by Bengie Molina, who is also from Puerto Rico. I was definitely okay with it. As a matter of fact, the next time I saw him, I walked right up and congratulated him because he had a great year, and when people have a great year, you have to shake their hand and say, "Keep it going, you're doing a good job." That's exactly what I told him. He deserved it.

Bengie's younger brother, Yadier, who plays for the St. Louis Cardinals, has won eight Gold Gloves on his own and is the best defensive catcher of his generation—hands down. He's going to be a Hall of Famer himself one day. If he stays healthy, he's going to be the next Puerto Rican catcher in Cooperstown. I hope he stays strong mentally and physically and I can one day watch him on the stage give his acceptance speech.

I had two goals each and every season of my career. One was to play in 150 games. Although I only did that twice, I came close a few other times. Secondly, I wanted to have a better season than the one before. Yeah, I know that was unrealistic as I got older, but that was always my goal until my last year.

As far as the awards, that's out of your control, you know? That was never a goal. I never went into a season wanting to win a Gold Glove, make an All-Star team, win a Silver Slugger, an MVP, Player of the Month, Player of the Week, etc. Since things like that were just out of my control, why focus on them? That's just counterproductive. There's nothing wrong with having goals, but they should be attainable through your own doing—not dependent on other people or those with a vote.

What was in my control was just playing hard every day. The Gold Gloves and Silver Sluggers, the MVP award—obviously—I appreciated the honors, but I'm going back to why I appreciated them. Because if I didn't work hard, the awards never would have come. Know how you always hear about all these young athletes with all this potential and then they disappear? That's the reason. Talent alone isn't the ticket. It's the hard work and dedication to their craft.

It was no secret that I wasn't likely returning to Texas, and the fans knew that, too. One of the really emotional moments of my career came in the last game of the 2002 season when I received a standing ovation from the home fans in all four of my at-bats against the Oakland A's. I was only supposed to hit three times. My third time up, there was a big ovation, and I hit a home run to left field. The game was stopped for a few minutes because of all the cheering from the crowd. I came out for a curtain call and waved to the fans. It was an incredible feeling. I love the Rangers fans so much, and this was where I grew up as a ballplayer. There were so many memories, so many emotions, so much appreciation on my end. I could have stayed there all day shaking hands with every single person in the stands. When I got back to the dugout, Jerry Narron asked me if I wanted to stay in the game. I said, "I want to go back out and catch. I want to go in for one more inning, then you can take me out if that's what you want to do."

Well, five guys hit after my home run the previous inning, so when Alex Rodriguez walked in the bottom of the eighth, I was due up again. I told hitting coach Rudy Jaramillo, "I want to hit one more time." He said, "No, man, stop right there. You just hit a home run." I said, "I don't care if I hit a home run. It's just one more time because I love this moment. I'm enjoying this moment. I want to make the fans happy one last time."

So, I went to Jerry and told him I wanted to hit one more time. On the first pitch I saw, I hit a double off the wall in right-center field. That was one of the best things that ever happened to me. Baseball is such an unbelievable game that sometimes you don't know what is going to happen. Look what happened with me— in my last two at-bats with the only franchise I played for, I hit a home run and then a double that almost went out of the ballpark. Make no mistake, if I could go back and relive three or four games of my baseball career, that game would definitely be on the list.

At first I was really heartbroken that I wouldn't be returning to the Rangers. I never really thought about playing with another team. To play your whole career with one organization, that was one of my main goals coming into the league. Even at the time,

I felt a great appreciation for the Rangers. There were never any negative feelings on my end. They gave me so much and really my opportunity to pursue my dream. And they made me an offer to stay—just not anywhere in the financial ballpark of what we were looking at, so it was time to look elsewhere. Only a few guys get to play their entire careers in one place anyway. Cal Ripken, Derek Jeter, Tony Gwynn, Craig Biggio, George Brett, Roberto Clemente, and Johnny Bench come to mind.

When I left I was second in franchise history in games played with 1,479, and that's just 33 fewer than another Gold Glove catcher, Jim Sundberg, a really good guy who still works in the team's front office. I was also first in hits with 1,723 and doubles with 344, second in runs with 852, third in RBIs with 829, and fourth in home runs with 215. No matter how my career finished up, I would always be a Texas Ranger.

Free agency was a new experience for me. There were only a few teams interested. I turned 31 that November and hadn't played more than 111 games in each of the previous three seasons. I'm sure a lot of folks figured I was done. My body was breaking down.

That was a tough offseason. I wasn't the first, second, or 100th free agent off the market. By January, when the overwhelming majority of free agents have signed, my offers were for three years, $18 million from the Baltimore Orioles and various deals from the Japanese League, which I wasn't really in a hurry to go to, but my agent, Jeff Moorad, was more than willing to listen to any and all offers.

There were a few other multi-year deals in the mix, too, but for some reason, I felt this powerful force telling me to sign with the Florida Marlins, who play in Miami where we had a home. My brother also lived there.

There's really no way for me to explain this. I just felt this positive vibe in playing with the Marlins. It just felt right, and I liked the idea of our family not having to uproot. And while we ended up being a great team, I wasn't sure what to expect. Then again, the year before the Rangers lost 90 games, and that was tough. I grew up on winning teams with the Rangers. And we hadn't won more than 73 games the previous three years.

The third week of January, somewhat out of nowhere, the Marlins called with a stronger interest than they had shown previously, which of course, made me quite happy. We were hoping for a five-year contract, but with my recent run of injuries and especially my back, well, they weren't interested in that.

When I did the physical, the doctor from Miami didn't want to approve the contract. He was telling owner Jeffrey Loria and general manager Larry Beinfest that if they did the deal, I might not finish the season because of the back issues. He said that he found something really bad in my back and he didn't want to approve the contract for the insurance policy or whatever. I was really frustrated.

The Marlins, though, still responded with a one-year offer for $10 million. For perspective of the time: it was one of the most frenzied free-agent offseasons in baseball history, and I was one of the four players to sign a deal for $10 million a year, joining Greg Maddux, Tom Glavine, and Jim Thome.

For me, it was a no-brainer. I wanted to play in Florida, I also wanted to prove to the baseball world that I was healthy and that my career wasn't winding down, I wanted to have one of the best years of my life. And it was great to be wanted, to be needed to lead a younger team. Loria said at the press conference announcing my signing, "We were dealing with a great and special opportunity to sign a special player. We feel like for our team this is a special year and a special season, and he warrants [spending the money]."

He couldn't have been more correct about it being a special season. Really, for so many of us, it was the season of a lifetime.

9

Forever a Champion

THE FLORIDA MARLINS WERE IN THEIR 11TH YEAR OF EXISTENCE when I joined them in 2003, and they had just one winning season to their credit. That one occasion came in 1997, when they earned a wild-card berth under manager Jim Leyland and stunned all of baseball by winning the World Series. Then they got rid of the majority of those players and went back to resembling an expansion franchise. Morale wasn't exactly high among the fanbase either. The year before my arrival they drew barely 10,000 fans per home game. Miami has a lot of hardcore baseball fans, but they want to root for a winner like anyone else.

There was a lot of young talent on that team, though, which was apparent from the first day of spring training. Derrek Lee, Luis Castillo, Juan Pierre, Juan Encarnacion, and Mike Lowell anchored the lineup, and all of them were in their 20s. Josh Beckett, Dontrelle Willis, Carl Pavano, Brad Penny, and Mark Redman made up the starting rotation, and all of them were also in their 20s. I was the old man at 31.

As I grew older, I talked with the younger guys all the time about respecting the game and playing the right way, but I never felt like the obvious team leader until that season with the Marlins. Probably part of that was my own maturity, and I was never the oldest starter on any of those Rangers teams.

So, while I was still intensely focused on my own game from the get-go, I felt like it was time to take my leadership to another level. I would talk to the younger players if they weren't showing respect or giving their best effort. I saw that a lot on my team, but I wasn't a player who would make a guy look bad in front of his teammates. I was calm. I would sit down after the game and talk a little bit about why they did what they did. It was tough because there are some players who just think they're the best. They think, *Who the fuck are you to tell me this?* Leave me alone. Sometimes you have to be careful. It backfired a few times with me. I would be calm and nice and sit down with a guy, and he would get mad at me and start to show me up. There were other ways I could have dealt with that, but honestly with those sort of players, that tended to work itself out. The game and the team environment usually weeds out those who don't commit themselves.

Beckett was just 23 years old, but what a talent he was. It was obvious why he was the second overall pick of the 1999 MLB Draft. And Willis, a left-hander, was 21. We called Miguel Cabrera up in June, and he was two months removed from turning 20. We were one of the youngest teams in the league. I loved it, though. I enjoyed seeing the energy that younger players bring and I enjoyed working with younger pitchers. I was beyond optimistic.

However, the season started really bad. It was a mess. We were a horrible baseball team there for a stretch. They fired Jeff Torborg as manager after a 16–22 start and replaced him with Jack McKeon, who was 72 but full of energy and positive thinking. He landed his first managerial job with the Kansas City Royals before the 1973 season, when I was one year old.

It wasn't an instant turnaround when Jack took over. We were still 34–39 on June 18, more than a month after the change. I had maybe the worst month of my career in May, hitting just

.169 as we lost 16 of our 28 games. We caught fire in mid-June, though, and won more than two-thirds of our remaining games. That year was really enjoyable for me because the younger players really listened to me, and I did my best to bring the leadership we needed. If you look back, a lot of those pitchers enjoyed one of the better years of their careers that season. We spent a lot of time before games going over scouting reports. We all enjoyed being at the park.

The chemistry changed almost instantly once Jack took over. And not only from our perspective either. Everyone suddenly wanted to go to Marlins games, we were playing before huge crowds, and the fans brought it every night and were as loud as possible. There are great baseball fans in the Miami area, many of them Hispanic, and they embraced that team. And we were able to accomplish something that none of them will ever forget.

Jack will always be "Cigar Man" to me; that's what I usually called him. He brought some real fire as a manager. He used to yell and scream in the dugout, and half the time we didn't even know who he was yelling at. Maybe it didn't matter. He just wanted us all to hear. He was the opposite of Jeff Torborg, who was a nice man, just laid-back. Jeff didn't say much and never raised his voice.

Jack was super intense. In the clubhouse he always was all over the place with a cigar and he would leave the cigar smell everywhere he went. When we were on the field, we all smelled like cigar smoke. But he was a great manager to play for. When he took over, we felt the change that first day—even if it took us a month or so to start winning. The atmosphere was the opposite of what it had been. He told me from the start, "I'm the manager, but you are the leader for me. So you go and take over the team."

I was glad when he said that, knowing he had my back if I needed to be in someone's face.

As was usually the case in my career, my bat came alive in the summer. In July I batted nearly .400 with 21 RBIs as we went 17–7. Around the time we clinched a wild-card berth, someone asked Atlanta Braves outfielder Gary Sheffield if he thought our team had snuck up on everyone. Gary, one of the better hitters in the game, had been a member of the 1997 Marlins World Series team. He said, "I don't see how. In spring training I said they were a good team. When they added Pudge, they added a guy with credibility."

Sheffield's Braves won 101 games and took our division, the National League East, but we felt some momentum entering the playoffs. There's nothing like a strong finish to bolster a team's confidence. The young staff and I didn't always agree on…well, just about everything. Willis went 14–6 and won NL Rookie of the Year, but the best of the bunch was Beckett. After the All-Star break, he posted a 2.55 ERA and struck out more than a batter per inning. With each start his stuff was improving.

JOSH BECKETT
MARLINS PITCHER
"When we signed Pudge, the atmosphere surrounding the franchise changed in an instant. I attended a FanFest event the night his signing was announced, and the Marlins were suddenly a big deal. It's all anyone could talk about. Pudge had this aura about him unlike anyone else. He wasn't just a star—he was a superstar, and that was exciting to be around. He made the rest of us believe that we belonged in the big leagues because we were on the same team as him. The season before, we would play a team and think, 'Look

at these guys, they're all probably driving fancy cars, and we always see them on *SportsCenter*.' But now, with Pudge it's, 'Hey, we can beat these guys.'

"Everyone talks about his arm, and they should, but he was such a great target behind the plate, one of the best receivers in the game, probably ever. Pudge kept his hands so still, which helps the pitcher relax, and he made adjustments during an at-bat, which few catchers do. We had a lot of confidence in the pitches he was calling because of his experience. Pudge would have been an unbelievable catcher even if he had the worst throwing arm in the league, never mind that he had the best."

The chemistry between Josh and me wasn't immediate because—well, as weird as this kind of sounds—I don't think the staff liked me all that much. Hopefully, in retrospect, they understand why I was the way I was that season. I wanted to win and I wanted to make them better. And both of those goals were accomplished. We can debate how big of a prick I was to them for the rest of our lives, but at least there was a means to an end.

I was talking to whoever the starting pitcher was from the moment he arrived in the locker room. I was putting scouting reports in his hands. We were meeting before batting practice for an hour and then again after. Maybe this wasn't the case early on, but as we started playing better, my intensity and thirst for success only increased.

What's truly amazing about what that staff accomplished that season was we lost our No. 1 starter, A.J. Burnett, for the season in April. He led the league in shutouts the year before and also had a no-hitter to his credit. What's also amazing is that every one of our starts, regular season and playoffs, came from guys in their 20s. That's unheard of.

If nothing else, I treated all the pitchers the same, really everyone on the team. I was everywhere that year. I wanted to be the first to the park even after my morning workouts. I was obsessed with maximizing this team's potential. Some of it was personal, too. A lot of front offices made something clear the previous offseason: the word around the league was that Pudge was finished. Trust me, as much as it hurt my ego, the phone wasn't ringing off the hook with offers, you know. This was my chance, and I was playing on a one-year deal. I was going to give all of myself to prove to them all that I wasn't ready for the twilight of my career, not by a longshot. So while the chemistry and relationship that I had with all of the pitchers was very good, I would make them mad sometimes. I thought, *I don't give a shit about you being a top prospect. You are a part of this team. And I know you're the top prospect, but you're in the big leagues now.*

And Josh and me, well, I would make him really pissed off. We're talking irate. Sometimes during the game, I would go straight to his face, right on the mound, and tell him, "You'd better get your ass going. This crap you're throwing wouldn't cut it in Little League. You're supposed to be this big-time pitcher, huh? I'm telling them to send you back to the bush leagues where you belong."

There was some colorful language mixed in. I'm sure you can use your imagination. I did it because I knew that he was going to be special. There's a difference between pushing a pitcher with decent stuff to have a good outing or whatever and pushing this 23-year-old with an arm from the baseball gods who could write his career. If Josh wanted to win Cy Young awards and World

Series MVP awards, he possessed that kind of talent. Not many pitchers have that.

Sometimes, you cannot babysit pitchers or players because if you do that, you're doing something bad for them. You are part of the problem. I was never a fan of coaches telling me what a great job I was doing. I knew the player I was, and their job was to push me to be better, to coach me to be better, to teach me something so I could improve.

And not only was I the veteran of the team, I was the only free-agent player the Marlins signed that year. It really was kind of bizarre that they came out of nowhere with that $10 million offer since they were really rebuilding the team with young, cheap talent. Everybody else was there the year before when they finished with a losing record.

I really thought about how the veteran players treated me with the Rangers back in the day, when I first came up and I was young. They were tough on me. They made sure I didn't think I was all that, that I wasn't a cocky kid who relied only on his talent.

That year with the Marlins, I would see all these young kids doing things they were not supposed to do. After the way that we started the season—we were still in last place in June—I said, "You know what? You'd better get going. If you want to be the No. 1 team, then act like the No. 1 team. Because right now you are not." I'd tell Josh, "You know, right now you are just shit, nothing more, nothing less."

They didn't appreciate it because they were young. They couldn't handle it. I can only imagine what they would say about me behind my back, especially when I was hitting like .240 at the end of May. *Tell the old man to shut up.* They thought that I was an asshole, but I really wasn't. With Josh I was his catcher and I wanted him to be great. I wanted him to dominate the league like he was capable of doing. That's the thing, if Josh was great, as we saw later that season, our team would be great, and we'd win.

If I'm being honest, I had a lot of issues at the time, too. For whatever reason I was never as tough on my teammates as that season. Not before with the Rangers and never going forward. Looking back, it was probably that one-year contract and the empty feeling of no one wanting me during the offseason. I mean, hell, I was considering going to Japan at one point. One minute, everyone is talking about me being headed to the Hall of Fame, the 10 straight Gold Gloves, the MVP award, and now I can't find a job in the big leagues at 31. That was a hit to the ego and carried over into the season.

It's just important to understand why I was like I was. Josh was a good kid and he probably didn't need me yelling at him every other pitch. Sometimes I would go to warm him up in the bullpen, and he would start doing stupid things. And I didn't like it. I would throw the ball back, screaming at him. And the next pitch he threw would be way up there. And I'm looking at him like, *Did you think you were going to do something to me with that? Are you trying to send a message?* And sometimes I would just get up, go back to the dugout, and let him find another catcher to get warmed up with. Know what, though, in those instances when I just walked away, he would always end up having a great game with me on the field.

One of the reasons all this happened on the Marlins that season, one of the main reasons that we had success was because I helped teach them how to be good pitchers. When I got to the Marlins, they were a bunch of throwers and—make no mistake— they had some incredible arms. Still, they were throwers, not pitchers. So, I made them be pitchers. I'd tell them, "Throw the ball right here, throw the ball right here, throw the ball right here.

Move it around, location, location, location. Be a pitcher." And if you look at the year before and compare it to 2003, the majority of them improved their earned run average and WHIP (walks and hits divided by innings pitched). Josh's ERA dropped more than a run—from 4.10 to 3.04. And he deserves a lot of the credit for that. I think I helped, too. I think they needed a veteran catcher. It also helped that my backup that season, Mike Redmond, was a veteran, a pro's pro. The front office did a nice job giving that young staff what it needed most in catchers.

My slow start meant I wasn't an All-Star for the second straight season. I also didn't win a Gold Glove, but my numbers ended up being pretty solid. I batted .297 and posted the second highest on-base percentage of my career at .369. I had a career-high 55 walks, hit 16 home runs, and drove in 85. I also hit 36 doubles, scored 90 runs, and stole 10 bases. Most importantly, I played in 144 games, matching the total from my MVP season four years earlier.

And I entered the postseason feeling pretty good. A lot of guys are banged up late in the year. That's where all my morning workouts made the difference. On the cusp of opening the playoffs against Barry Bonds and the San Francisco Giants, my skipper removed his cigar from his mouth long enough to tell the media, "Pudge, he's back to his All-Star status again. He's playing remarkably well. He's been a take-charge guy, a leader of the ballclub."

And we were just getting started.

When I was with the Rangers, I am pretty sure no one held any individual player responsible for losing those three division series to the New York Yankees from 1996 to 1999. We came up against the greatest team of the generation, we just weren't good enough, and we had to tip our caps. They went on to win all three of those World Series, too. I did okay in those 10 playoff games, batting .263 with three RBIs and playing solid defense. But to become one of those guys who is remembered when your grandchildren talk to their grandchildren, well, you need to leave a mark in the postseason.

And I fully intended on taking advantage of my most recent opportunity.

Still today, I can't believe that we won that year because of the teams we played against. I'm talking about facing the Giants in the best-of-five division series, being able to eliminate them when they had a monster team that won 100 games during the regular season. They had Benito Santiago behind the plate, J.T. Snow at first base, and, of course, Bonds in the outfield.

We had lengthy scouting reports on every hitter and pitcher on the Giants except one—Bonds. We literally did not have a scouting report for him. We didn't talk about him for more than a few seconds before the series and each game. There was no reason to discuss him further. How were we going to pitch to Bonds? Just like everyone else did during those years. We were going to walk him. I'm not kidding either. We did not have a scouting report. It was the only time in my career we didn't even bother having a report on a hitter. If someone took the time to write up a report, which I never saw, here's what it would've said: "If you don't have to pitch to him—meaning it's not bases loaded in a tie game in the ninth inning—put him on first base. If you need to pitch to him, our deepest sympathies. And don't strain a neck muscle or anything turning around."

I'm laughing right now just thinking about pitching to him at that point. It was a joke. If the strike was in his zone, it was gone. And he mastered the strike zone unlike anyone ever has. For the five-year stretch of 2000–04, Barry's on-base percentage was .535, and he hit 258 home runs. He got on base in nearly 54 percent of his plate appearances for half a decade. They don't let you do that in video games. From those three seasons of 2002 to 2004—despite missing 66 games over that stretch—he walked 578 times. I played 21 seasons and walked 513 times.

If the bases were empty, I can promise you this: if one of my pitchers threw him a strike, he missed his spot. We were throwing around him, and more times than not, I was just standing up and pointing my arm out. Barry came to the plate 18 times in the four-game series and walked eight times, including six intentionally. He went 2-for-9 with a sacrifice fly, a double, and a single in those other plate appearances. I considered that the biggest win imaginable.

We were not going to give him anything to hit. We might have thrown him one hittable pitch near the strike zone, but that sucker didn't swing. He was so focused and just wanted the one pitch he was looking for. That's why he walked 148 times that season and 232 times the following year because his eyes were so in tune, waiting for that pitch. That's what is unbelievable to me. Think about it: he might only see the pitch he's waiting for once on a given night and he's not going to miss it. He's going to hit it out of the ballpark. He was walked more than 2,500 times in his career and he ended up hitting 762 home runs. It's amazing.

Was Barry the best hitter I ever played with or against? He's definitely one of the best. Manny Ramirez was also one of the best and so were Vladimir Guerrero and Andres Galarraga. Manny had quick hands. What Manny did that was very, very good was he was always on time. His front foot always landed on time, and the ball was still a good distance from the plate. That's why he was able to see every single pitch and just pull it. Now, if you saw Manny Ramirez in batting practice, he was hitting balls out of the ballpark the other way. There was nothing that man couldn't do with a baseball bat.

Jason Schmidt outdueled Josh in Game 1, an old-school, pitching-dominated game, which we lost 2–0. We took Game 2 in San Francisco and returned to a raucous Pro Player Stadium for Game 3. That place was rocking, nearly 62,000 strong. I hit a two-run homer in the first inning, and the Giants plated two in the sixth, which was all the scoring until the 11th inning, when San Francisco scored the go-ahead run on a walk, an error, and a single.

The game was more than four hours old when I came to the plate in the bottom half of the 11th with two outs and the bases loaded. This was what every kid who ever played baseball dreams about. The count went to 1–2, and Tim Worrell threw me a tailing fastball, a little high, a little outside. It was the perfect location to use all those lessons from my old hitting coach Rudy Jaramillo and just go with the pitch, take it to right, which I did. I smashed a line drive between the first and second basemen, two runners scored, and we won 4–3. I remember rounding first base as the throw came home and watching Juan Pierre—one of the fastest guys in the game—slide headfirst to easily beat it, then raising my helmet in the air as my teammates rushed toward me to celebrate. When my teammates finally gave me a second to break free, I spiked the helmet into the dirt. It was my own little touchdown celebration. When asked about the game afterward, Pierre told the media, "Pudge put us on his back—simple as that."

It's even more magical than you dream it will be. Time really does kind of stop for that instant with the fans screaming and your teammates going crazy. I really wish everyone who loves the game could experience that one time. That was without question the most clutch hit of my career.

However, it wasn't the most clutch play of my career. That came the very next day.

In the bottom of the eighth inning of Game 4, I scored the go-ahead run with Derrek Lee seconds behind me for a 7–5 lead. Our closer, Ugueth Urbina, struggled in the ninth, and suddenly it was a one-run game. The Giants had runners on first and second with two outs. Jeffrey Hammonds singled, a dying flare that wasn't hit hard, to left field. Veteran Jeff Conine fielded it cleanly in left and came up firing to home, and Snow hustled down the line, right at me. I fielded it on one clean bounce in front and just to the left of the plate. Snow was still several strides from reaching me or home. As I shifted in front of the plate and in front of him, it quickly became obvious that there was only one way this was going to end—with Snow, whose father was an NFL wide receiver, giving his all to knock the ball loose from my grip. We had a collision, and while he knocked me to the ground, he wasn't able to knock the ball free. I tumbled backward and raised the ball toward the heavens. As the umpire emphatically signaled out, Urbina jumped on top of me, and the place went nuts. There were so many plays over my career, but if I could relive one, that would be it, which is really saying something because J.T. hit me pretty good.

In defeating the Giants, I came to the plate 20 times and reached base nine. I also had a series-best six RBIs and two game-ending plays.

We were going to the National League Championship Series. Our opponents were the Chicago Cubs, who were trying to win their first league title since 1945 and their first World Series since 1908. The American League Championship Series was the

Boston Red Sox and the Yankees—perhaps the fiercest rivalry in any sport, never mind just baseball. This was October baseball at its finest. Both series went the distance, too.

We won Game 1 at Wrigley 9–8 in 11 innings. I hit a three-run homer off Carlos Zambrano in the third and finished with five RBIs. Lowell hit the game-winning home run in the 11th. Josh started and didn't have his best stuff, allowing four runs in the first inning and six total. The Cubs won the next three games, though, and when we took the field for Game 5 in Miami, I don't think there was anyone who thought we were going to win that series. At least not outside of our locker room.

But Josh was on the hill and he was brilliant. He threw a complete-game shutout, allowed just two hits, and struck out 11. I was able to hit another home run, and we were headed back to Chicago.

BECKETT

"I got my ass kicked in Game 1, and then we had our brains beat in for three games. It was not looking promising. That first start, Pudge and I were having some issues. He was yelling at me for shaking off signs, and I told him he was calling different signs than what we went over. I told him in the second inning, 'I'm really pissed at you right now,' and he said, 'Good because I'm pissed at you.' A few other words might have been involved. We were damn lucky to win that game or we would have been swept.

"For Game 5 he was yelling at me in the bullpen, reminding me not to fly open during my delivery. I remember thinking I was throwing hard out there, and he's throwing the ball back to me even harder with no windup. You look back now and appreciate the way his leadership came out again and again that entire postseason. That was his deal. Pudge was leading that whole deal. And he was dealing with a bunch of kids on the staff, too.

"When Kerry Wood hit that home run in Game 7, that's the loudest I've ever heard a park in my life. We eventually were down 5–3, and Pudge is yelling at us to play nine innings, to forget the home run, and just play nine innings. His focus never wavered even in that environment."

We were trailing 3–0 in the eighth inning of Game 6 in Chicago when the Steve Bartman play happened, involving that poor fan in the stands who did what any of us would have and tried to catch the ball above Moises Alou. It's ridiculous that one play is remembered. I mean, we scored eight runs that inning, and the entire world blames some accountant listening to the game on the radio.

The Cubs had two absolute studs in Mark Prior and Kerry Wood, but they were both tired as they went later into games. There were a lot of innings for those young arms, and we chased Prior in the eighth to force a Game 7. Our young hitting star, Cabrera, launched a three-run homer in the first, and while Chicago came back with five runs, we kept hitting. Josh came in from the bullpen to throw four heroic innings before Urbina closed out the 9–6 win. I was named the series MVP, leading all players with 10 RBIs and reaching base 14 times.

MIGUEL CABRERA
MARLINS OUTFIELDER
"When I came up in June, it was clear from my first minute there, this was Pudge's team. We looked to him and tried to do like he told us. If we did something that was out of line or

he disagreed with, he was sure to tell us. I learned so much from him that year. He kind of took me under his wing and taught me the right way to play, how to respect the game, my teammates, how to carry myself. Pudge was everything to me that season. I admire him so much, and it was such an honor to play with him and have the success we did."

The Yankees won a thrilling seven-game series of their own, and there I was again in Yankee Stadium in the postseason. This time, though, we were where no one expected us to be—in the Fall Classic. I used to watch television back in Puerto Rico with my family when Johnny Bench played in the World Series and now I was joining my childhood hero in doing so.

Following a 3–2 win in Game 1, in which I picked off Nick Johnson at third base when he was the go-ahead run, we lost back-to-back games by the same score of 6–1. Game 4 at home was going to be key to the series either way. I didn't know if we could come back from another 3–1 deficit and I didn't want to find out. The game went more than four hours before Alex Gonzalez homered to lead off the bottom of the 12th. We won again the following night 6–4 and headed back to the Bronx, needing one win for the title. There is no bigger stage in baseball than Yankee Stadium.

And Josh Beckett was on the hill for Game 6.

No more than four Yankees came to the plate in any of the nine innings. Josh was masterful, throwing a five-hit shutout as we won 2–0. He was named World Series MVP, and I was a world champion. No matter what the remainder of my life would bring, no one could ever take that away. We were World Series champs.

BECKETT

"There was no shaking him off that day. Not once. All three pitches were working, including backdoor curveballs to right-handed hitters, front-door sliders at 97, 98 miles per hour. While everyone was celebrating in the clubhouse, frankly, I was tired, exhausted really, and I was wearing this ugly ass jacket someone gave me. I made my way into the kitchen, off the locker room, and Pudge walks in behind me with two beers. He handed me one, and said, 'Can you believe it?' I still have that jacket just because of that moment.

"We see each other every year out in Lake Tahoe for a golf tournament plus here and there on other occasions, and it's never a handshake. It's a hug that couldn't be more heartfelt. We bonded that year in a way that's impossible to explain. We were all talking about the next season, trying to win it again, and they broke us all up a month later. That was unbelievable. That sucked—only having that one season with Pudge."

After the final out in Game 6, I told him, "We did it. I don't know if we're going to do it again, but we did it." He came in with three days' rest for that game. When we sat down beforehand and looked at the scouting report, we went briefly through all the hitters. And basically what I told him was, "Look, enjoy this. We only have 27 more outs to go, then we can go home and rest. Can you do that?" He said, "I'm ready to do it." And that was the conversation.

He was nasty that day, better than three days earlier. He threw it even harder. He was throwing steady at 98 to 99 miles per hour. His fastballs didn't go down below that, but his pitches were hitting wherever I set up my glove—inside corner, outside corner, again and again. Nothing right down the middle. And his curveballs were perfect. The Yankees didn't stand a chance.

To me, Josh was the best double-up pitcher I ever caught or saw. Do you know what double-up means? Say, for example, that the pitcher starts with a breaking ball for a ball. I call double-up, which means I call for it again. And it's a high percentage that the second pitch is going to be a strike. In some hitters' heads, if you start with a breaking ball, they think you're not going to repeat it because the fastball is the pitch that the pitcher has the most control of. So, the hitters are thinking, *He's not going to throw me a breaking ball again because if it's a ball I'm going to be ahead in the count 2–0. He's going to throw me a heater, and I'm going to be ready for it.* And that pitch, that double-up, can often be a pitcher's best friend because the pitcher has to focus more on that breaking ball the second time around. It's about a 90 percent chance that the second pitch, which is a double-up, is going to be a strike.

If I started with a breaking ball with Josh, I called for it again, and he'd throw it for a strike. Every time. He was very good about that. If I called for a fastball in on the first pitch and went back in there, it was perfect. I loved catching him that postseason. Our relationship evolved over those eight months, going back to spring training. He's one of my favorite teammates, even though we spent just the year together. Josh is a big reason I was able to accomplish my ultimate dream.

In the clubhouse while I was drenched in champagne, a reporter asked me about the future. Without hesitation I said, "Our clubhouse, my teammates, we're very united. Nobody knows what is going to happen next year, but my personal opinion is this team will stay together for many years to come. If this team stays together the way it is, I think we can be like the Yankees. We can win probably pretty much every year."

Well, I was right about not knowing what was going to happen.

10

A New Home

THAT OFFSEASON SHOULD HAVE BEEN GLORIOUS, AND IN MANY ways, it was. We took a few family vacations, went to Italy, spent some time in Venice, and I woke up every morning thinking, *Yes, I am now a world champion.* Nothing beats that. There was just one problem.

I was unemployed.

The gamble I took on myself paid off. Having proven not only that my baseball skills were sharp as ever, I also showed that I was still healthy, durable, and a good leader. I wanted a lengthy contract in the offseason. I went back to Scott Boras as my agent after winning the World Series. I had also started my career with him. During my whole career, I always had good relationships with my agents, guys like Jeff Moorad and Mike Fiore, but for this important of a contract, in many ways the most important of my life, I wanted Scott.

I was 32 years old, which seemed old to many—at least by catching standards. But I felt great and felt like I had some of the best seasons of my life ahead. That was a long offseason, though, and that's after playing most of October in the postseason.

I wasn't leaning toward any one team when the free agency process began in November 2003. Obviously, it would have been great to stay in Florida because we would be coming back as the defending champs. I also would have enjoyed another year at home. Even when I was with the Rangers, we spent part of the offseason in Miami.

The Marlins offered me two years at the same money I made the year before, which was $10 million per year. They wanted to pay me the same contract with no raise and for only two years. I was furious. To me, that was a slap in the face. It didn't show any commitment. Really, it was almost like them saying, "Hey, thanks for the memories, see you later."

And all the players were mad because of how well we bonded. We wanted to stay together and see if we could have a little run of success. The fans were upset, too. The front office just gutted the team. They wouldn't spend any money. Are you telling me they didn't make a few bucks winning the World Series the season before? Of course they did and they could have put that money back into the team. Instead they traded Derrek Lee and didn't sign any of their free agents. They haven't returned to the playoffs since.

There were a bunch of new players on the team for Opening Day, not the players who won the World Series and deserved a chance to defend the title. Just imagine how bad it looks to have so many new players when you're the defending champions. It was the same thing they did in 1997, when Wayne Huizenga was owner. They were a pretty decent team when new owner John Henry, who now owns the Boston Red Sox, bought the team in 1999. Dave Dombrowski was the general manager. Fans in Miami love their baseball, and I saw that in the short time I played there. Baseball is a business, though. Sometimes you don't know when it's going to be the last day you're going to be on that team. So, you always have to be prepared for anything. And I mean anything.

Since I was a free agent, Scott and I were having constant conversations. When we were dealing with a team, he would tell me what their meetings were all about, what they discussed, what kind of deal they wanted, whether it was a short or long-term deal, etc. That's a constant when you go through free agency. Nothing happens until Scott starts talking to teams. Normally right after the season, ballclubs and agents don't talk to each other. You always take about a month or month and a half off before the winter meetings begin in December.

I would have some input, but it's not like I was telling Scott I wanted to play for certain teams. That's because you never know who you're going to play for. For example, do you think I had in mind that I'd be playing with Detroit after I won the World Series with Florida the year before? There you go. I thought I was going to stay in Florida and I ended up playing with Detroit. You just never know.

Surprise calls came in at the last minute. And when I signed with Detroit, there were other teams that were involved, but they weren't offering the multi-year contract I wanted. There were a lot of one-year and two-year offers with an option. I'm like, "Okay, just keep going, keep going" until almost spring training, when Detroit called. Dombrowski, the former Marlins GM who took the Tigers job a few years earlier, called Scott and said, "Look, I want Pudge to become a Tiger."

That was in February, which is really late for a free agent.

The other teams in the mix were the Chicago Cubs, Seattle Mariners, and Baltimore Orioles. Again, none were going to be for more than two years.

And it's not like we were asking for too much money. The teams we were talking to agreed we weren't asking for crazy money. They were just worried about my back. Word had leaked, as it always does, around the league that the Marlins were worried about my back from the physical the year before. It felt fine, but obviously everyone remembered me missing two months during my final year with the Rangers.

The deal we were hoping for kind of came out of nowhere. It also became really complex and frustrating. I was in Puerto Rico when I got that call. Scott said, "Hey, I've got good news for you. Detroit called." I said, "What? Detroit?" He said, "Yeah, yeah, I know, I know. But I think this is the best choice for you because I was talking to Dave, and he wants to build a good team around you." And I liked that. When he told me that, I said, "Wow, okay. What are the terms of the contract?" He said, "Four years, $40 million with an option for a fifth."

I responded, "Okay, so when are we going?"

We flew up to Detroit, and everyone was in agreement on the contract. I'm sure Scott was just negotiating because that's what he's supposed to do, but I was fine with the initial offer. I just needed to take the physical before putting ink to paper.

Sounds easy enough, right?

The Tigers doctors weren't thrilled with my back. They didn't want to approve the contract. They said, "If Pudge plays two years, it's going to be a lot. He's probably not even going to play one more year." And I looked at Dave and I said, "You know, Dave, I heard that last year." And he wanted to get the deal done regardless, so we rewrote the contract. We waited for two weeks as the player's union read it over because it was a unique deal in that I was giving up guaranteed money. Once again, I was betting on myself.

I knew I was healthy. I knew I could play the five years, depending on if they picked up the option. And I played eight more years after that. I mean, the doctors can tell you whatever they want to say, but it's how you feel that counts.

Within hours of the deal being announced, Scott and I were receiving phone calls by the dozen from friends, baseball people, and the media. They all had the same question: what is Pudge doing? Has he lost his mind? Who wins the World Series and then signs with a team that just lost 119 games? Those 119 losses were just one off the modern-day record set by the 1962 expansion New York Mets. The Tigers hadn't even finished with a winning record in a decade, going back to the days of the great manager Sparky Anderson. So, there was nothing wrong with anyone asking that question, and I understood why they were asking. My answer was pretty simple. I said, "Well, that was last year, and I wasn't on the team that lost all those games. And I have no plans on losing anywhere near that many in any year I'm on the team."

Know what else? I love a challenge. We had a few teams involved and offering deals, but Dave, one of the best in the game, promised me before I signed that we would compete for a championship within a few years. I believe his exact words were: "Pudge, give me two years, and that third season, we'll be in the World Series. With you on board, a lot of great players are going to want to play for the Tigers."

He was right. Others came on board, too. I guess it was like *Field of Dreams*. If you sign one crazy player, others will come. Dombrowski spoke about my situation to the *Detroit Free Press* in January 2017: "It was an unusual situation in that he wasn't somebody we pursued right off the bat. We've talked about it a lot. To me, that was the definitive moment in the build-back of the Tigers organization at that time. The start of it was Pudge joining us. Because with a guy like Pudge Rodriguez, when he joined the Tigers, then it also opened up other people's minds to say, 'Hey, if Pudge will come, then maybe we should consider it.' Also, we had the chance to see one of the best players of his generation play every day. That was pretty special in and of itself."

I'm not going to lie—and I've already mentioned this in passing earlier in the book—I am not a huge fan of cold weather. I'm from Puerto Rico and played the first 13 years of my big league career in Texas and Florida. Those are the only three places I ever called home, too. And now I was moving to Michigan, where it snows. I don't like temperatures in the 50s, never mind snow. Still, it was really only April when it was chilly. I wasn't spending offseasons there; it was back to Miami and Puerto Rico.

I actually came to love Detroit. I bought a house in Bloomfield Hills and made some lifelong friends. I never went out, so I couldn't really speak about the nightlife. As with my previous stops, during the baseball season I was at the park, at my house, in my car, or on a road trip. That was it. You would never find me anywhere else. I had my own personal chef, so I was never eating out either. I was focused on baseball and spending what little time was left with my family.

Detroit is an incredibly loyal baseball city. The fans adore their team and support them as much as any city in the game. And Comerica Park is fantastic. It's a wonderful place to play and watch baseball. Each of my last two seasons with the Tigers, we drew more than three million fans, and the TV ratings were always high. They love all sports in Detroit but especially baseball. I really enjoyed living there.

Let me be honest. The No. 1 reason I signed with Detroit was the four-year offer. Players can try and say it's not about the money and security, but that's important. That's our livelihood— just like anyone with their job. If you are a fireman and your hometown fire department offers you a job, and the town next door doubles that salary, I am pretty sure everyone is taking the extra money.

Also, it's worth mentioning that I earned $50 million in my years with Detroit, so taking the risk on myself paid off. Despite everything that was written into that contract to protect them from my supposed back issues, I met every clause and earned every dime. In fact, one could make the case that was the healthiest five-year stretch of my career, even though I was in my mid-30s.

My manager was Alan Trammell, a fantastic player himself for the Tigers for 20 years who should be in the Hall of Fame. We got along beautifully. We really had no issues. He let me do my thing, and there was a lot of mutual respect there. We actually played against each other the last six years of his career.

That first season in 2004, we won 29 more games than the season before, and I finished in the top 10 of the American League MVP voting for the fourth time in the previous nine years. I batted .334, which was fourth in the league and the highest of my career, among seasons in which I had enough plate appearances to qualify for the hitting crown. I also hit 19 home runs, won my 11th Gold Glove (my first in three years), and was the starting catcher in the All-Star Game (also for the first time in three years).

More importantly, though, our promising first year of the turnaround attracted Magglio Ordonez to sign with us in the offseason. He was among the better hitters in the league. He's right there with Juan Gonzalez for the best I ever played with in terms of hitting the baseball.

However, signing Magglio was really the only good news of my offseason. It was a nightmare. I already talked about this some in the first chapter, but I want to make sure everyone understands why I dropped around 30 pounds that winter. I feel like if I was more open and honest about it, then maybe the questions would have been answered, and that nonsense would have stopped there.

When the 2004 season ended, Maribel and I separated. We had been together for 18 years and married since 1992. That's why I came in the following year so skinny. I was very fit, too, weighing about 190 or 195 pounds. But sometimes the fans and other people don't understand when athletes are going through problems like that off the field, especially what I went through since it took me almost three years to finish that whole divorce situation.

And it wasn't easy. But the good thing was that I left all my problems away from the ballpark. I left all the problems in the car or at the house. When I went to the ballpark, I was totally focused on my job. The outside stuff never bothered me. Trust me: those were two or three of the best seasons I had in my career because I was focused so much on what I needed to do on the field. Then when I left the field it was like, "Okay, I'm going back to being a normal person and facing this tough situation."

During that offseason it was hard because I was leaving the house and my three kids, who were very close to me. When I was at the house, we would watch movies or jump on the boat and go for boat rides around Florida. And I wasn't able to do that anymore. I had to force myself to leave the house and go get an apartment. I would be by myself and think about the many, many things that you go through when you're alone. I didn't like to be by myself, but I forced myself to do it. That's part of life, and trust me: I learned so much from that. Sometimes you have to go through things in life that are hard, but you learn a lot from those things.

I just made myself focus on training, and my trainer and I started to work hard and ride bicycles in the mornings. I got to a point where I was riding 150 miles four times a week. At one point I rode from Key Biscayne all the way to Key Largo twice a week. I would just get off the bike there and drive back, which could take more than an hour. So, that tells you how focused I was and how I could put everything else aside and just ride bikes. It was just go, go, go. It even got to a point where my trainer, Edgar Diaz, told me that what I was doing was wrong. One time he took the bike from me. It just disappeared one day. Edgar wanted to be doing our old workouts of lifting weights and running. I didn't want to do any of that. I wanted to ride my bike and be alone in my thoughts. Of course, I still love riding bikes. I just ride them like a normal person now—not like I'm training for the Tour de France.

But going back to that situation, I was disappointed when I came to spring training in 2005. They saw that I was skinny, and then all these rumors started to come in. Most of the journalists just assumed stuff; they never came and talked to me. I've never turned down a question from a journalist. I understood they were part of the game and I respected the job they had to do.

Also, I didn't want everyone to know what I was going through, which is why I didn't exactly speak up about it. I've always been a private guy, especially with my family. But I had the answer as to why I was skinnier and I was waiting to throw it out there. I don't want anybody to go through what I went through. I did a TV interview with a lady in Spanish and, when we started talking about it, I made her cry with how sad my life was that offseason. But anyway, that's part of life. Maribel and I are both doing okay now. We both remarried, and I wish her happiness.

That 2005 season was disappointing. We had some injuries and didn't really improve from the previous year. I didn't have my best season, and Alan was fired. I felt horrible about that, but I was pretty excited about who the Tigers hired as his replacement because from everything I heard we had just landed one of the better managers in the game.

And he was that and a whole lot more.

Jim Leyland was the manager who I respected the most during my career. That was because of the way he was with me, the way he managed, and the way he loved the team he was leading. He was very intense, a brilliant in-game manager who took care of and supported his players every single time. To me, there was no better manager at defending his players than Jim. If, for example, someone from the media made a comment about a player and he didn't like it or thought it was unfair, he'd get mad and start to argue with whoever said or wrote it. Jim went to bat for his players, and that goes a long way. Honestly, I think Jim stuck up for his players even when he didn't entirely agree with their beef, but again he wanted us to know he had our backs.

I loved the chemistry he instilled, too. He was very approachable in the clubhouse, in the dugout, on the plane, or on the bus. He wanted to be like one of us in terms of being able to have a conversation and talk about life. He was never above us; he was one of us. I played for some great managers in my career, but Jim taught me the most about being a team leader and not straying away from that. He said, "You've got a good team. You're my player, and I want you to play hard every day for me and for the Tigers."

He was pretty calm on the field, but he could become really mad in the clubhouse. When things weren't going well, he didn't wait too long to let us know he was upset. And we respected that. We had a great team when he arrived, and Jim was the final piece. We needed somebody like that to tell us to wake up and play baseball. He told us the truth. He was an incredibly honest person. He told you things whether you liked them or not. And that's why I liked him so much.

At his core, though, Jim is a very kind, sensitive person and, if he felt something, he would show it. He would tell you what he thought was the best for you. We had some meaningful one-on-one conversations, talking baseball in the office, on the field, or in batting practice. We had a great relationship, and I talked to him a lot during our time together.

That 2006 season just felt different from the start. Maybe it was Jim coming in. We just felt like we were ready to compete for a playoff berth even in spring training. Magglio was healthy. I felt great, the pitching staff was dramatically improved with rookie Justin Verlander, and my old friend, Kenny Rogers, joined us. The guy was 41 years old but pitching some of the best ball of his career. He won 17 games for us, posted a solid 3.84 ERA, and, most importantly, gave the team 200-plus quality innings.

Verlander was throwing some gas from the start. His stuff—and I don't use this word often—was electric. He was throwing 100 miles per hour to begin with, but his pitches almost always had movement, too. Natural movement. If he stayed healthy, there was no doubt in my mind he was going to win a Cy Young. And he did in 2011. Really, he could easily have three or four right now because he's come in second twice and third another time.

JUSTIN VERLANDER
TIGERS PITCHER
"I remember the first time he caught me at my first camp as a rookie. He was kind of standing off to the side watching

our throwing sessions, and I was looking out of the corner of my eye like, 'Holy shit, that's Pudge.' Finally, he tapped the catcher on the side and said he wanted to catch some of my pitches. So I'm there in the bullpen, 22 years old, throwing as hard as I can, trying to impress Pudge. He catches a few pitches and says, 'Alright. I got him. Good job.' That was pretty special.

"He was a great teammate who not only led by example, but he was also vocal. One of the great things about him is that he wasn't afraid to tell guys if they were doing something the wrong way, which is an attribute I think is needed, especially with a bunch of younger guys in the clubhouse like we had. When Pudge first came over in 2004, that had a big effect on a lot of guys. As a batterymate, what can you say? You trust him. He's been around for a long time and he's one of the best of all time to do it. So it was pretty comforting as a rookie to have him behind the plate."

Really, the key that season was the pitching staff. Jeremy Bonderman struck out more than 200 batters, and Nate Robertson really had a nice year. The bullpen was stacked, too. Todd Jones had 37 saves, and set-up man Joel Zumaya, well, I honestly don't even know how to explain what that guy was throwing. I thought Nolan Ryan was zipping in some fastballs, but this Zumaya dude was throwing 106 with a nasty slider. No pitcher has ever thrown to me harder than he did. My hand hurts just thinking about that guy.

We started the season with five straight wins and never really looked back. On April 5 against Kansas City, I went 5-for-5, the only time I did that in my career. I had three doubles and a home run, and we beat the Royals 14–3.

That was a fun year, one of my favorite seasons. We went 95–67, which was good for a wild-card berth. At 34 years old, I was voted a starter for the All-Star team, won my 12th Gold Glove, batted .300 for the 10th and final time, and even played a position besides catcher for the first time. I started seven games at first base and played two innings at second base that August against the Boston Red Sox. I even caught a pop fly.

We had a chance to win the division on the final day of the season, but we lost in extra innings, which gave the Minnesota Twins the title. I reached base all six times I came to the plate that game in the 10–8, 12-inning loss to Kansas City and had three hits and three walks. See, I walked sometimes.

Although the loss was disappointing, we still achieved our ultimate goal of securing a postseason berth. And you'll never guess who our opponent was for the divisional round. Yes, the New York Yankees. Again. This was my fifth and last trip to the playoffs in my career, and every time I played against New York.

We dropped Game 1 at Yankee Stadium 8–4 but tied the series with a gutsy 4–3 win in Game 2. Back in Detroit Kenny threw a gem, allowing just five hits and striking out eight during seven and two-thirds shutout innings. He was a month shy of turning 42. We beat Randy Johnson and the Yankees 6–0 to go up two games to one. Randy was 43 by then, so that has to be one of the oldest postseason pitching matchups in baseball history. Randy was nasty in his prime. Just filthy. And at 6'10" with those long arms, that ball came down on you quick.

I'll tell you something else. That bullpen session Kenny threw before that game was quite possibly the worst bullpen I've seen a pitcher have. I'm not exaggerating. He didn't throw a single strike. It was a mess. I thought there was something wrong with him. I was expecting a horror show and I wasn't even sure he could make it out of the first inning. That's baseball for you; you just never know.

The series was closed out in Game 4 as we rolled 8–3. I had two RBIs, and Magglio set the tone with an early home run. And everyone thought I was crazy signing with the Tigers. Here we were about to play the Oakland A's for the American League crown.

Sometimes, though not often in the postseason, one team just catches a break here or there, and what was supposed to be a highly competitive series turns out completely different. That was the case for us. Placido Polanco batted .529 over the four-game sweep for MVP honors, and Kenny, my word, Kenny was having a postseason for the ages. He had another scoreless start, throwing seven and one-third innings of two-hit ball in Game 3.

For the second time in my career, I was headed to the World Series. And we were favored to win it all, as our opponents, the St. Louis Cardinals, won just 83 games in the regular season, though that was enough to win their division. That's just one more than the fewest wins in baseball history for a team that made the postseason. Still, they got hot when it mattered most.

We split the first two games in Detroit, and Kenny again was just masterful. This time he threw eight shutout innings, meaning he threw 23 scoreless in the playoffs.

KENNY ROGERS
TIGERS PITCHER

"I loved having Pudge again in Detroit. Our relationship was like we had never left. I mean, I was pitching pretty good, even though I was getting older, but it was still a fun relationship and it was a calming influence to be able to have a guy that you pitched to for years and years that understood what you're capable of and your style.

"I think those were three different types of games that postseason. I tried to change my MO and all. With him he grew up with me, too. When I was younger, I threw hard and I didn't know how to pitch. As I evolved as a pitcher, he was there and saw it, which was good. That made all the difference for me.

"I know the Yankees game, I changed my whole MO. It was as hard as I could possibly throw. I had other stuff, but every fastball was 100 percent effort. And that was just like when I was younger. I didn't have 100 percent control back then, but I threw at 100 percent effort. In that game I had control. But that was that style of game because they had been hitting me pretty well [earlier in the season], and Pudge understood it. He called such a brilliant game.

"Well, the next game against Oakland, I had to go back to doing what I normally did, and again Pudge was calling all the pitches. I don't think I shook him off once. It was three different games, but we were right in sync the whole time in all of them. I wish I'd had gotten another start. I think we would have done well.

"Having Pudge behind the plate, that gave me as a pitcher all the confidence in the world. He was just at another level than any other catcher, at least that I ever saw. He's the best."

The three games back in St. Louis were a nightmare. We dropped all three by the respective scores of 5–0, 5–4, and 4–2. If we just could have won a game, Kenny was pitching Game 6 back in Detroit. And then if he keeps rolling, anything can happen in a

Game 7. It just wasn't meant to be. There's really nothing else for me to say about those games. We should have won that year, and I'm still upset about it all these years later. Winning one World Series was an incredible, life-changing experience, so winning a second one really would have been special.

At the time I remember thinking that the lone bright spot was that we were young (well, outside of Kenny and me) and that we could definitely be back there the next season. But a lot has to go right for that to happen.

11

Umpires and the Empire Cty

EVERYONE KNOWS THAT I WAS AN INTENSE PLAYER. I WORE MY emotions on my sleeve, as the expression goes. When I was excited, I often pumped my fist and yelled in joy. When I was angry, I tended to showcase those emotions, too. I think my temperament helped me as a player since my natural intensity made me who I was. Still, there are times I wish I was able to keep it under control a little better. You would think that after playing baseball for more than 30 years, I would have learned to accept making outs. As we all know, the most successful hitters to ever step into a batter's box fail seven out of 10 times. Think about that. Name one other job in the world where you fail that much and are considered a success. If a basketball player misses seven of 10 shots, they are out of a job. Same for a quarterback throwing passes.

Still, I couldn't deal with it. Of the 6,748 times I went to the plate and failed to deliver a hit, a walk, a hit by pitch, a sacrifice bunt, or a sacrifice fly, I was probably upset every time. I probably swore every single instance, too, as I likely did on a few of those 58 times I was hit by pitches. Those hurt, though I never let the pitchers see that. There were a few times I even picked up the ball and tossed it back to them.

So yes, I became really angry when I made an out. The way I look at it: if you don't get mad, it's because you don't care. If I made an out, I was not happy. My batting helmets definitely have some battle stories to tell. I would often go behind the dugout where there's a storage area and take my frustration out there.

In 2007, my fourth full season in Detroit, I was ejected from two games by the men in blue. This was happening more than it used to. My first 10 seasons, I was ejected only once. That's pretty good for 1,300 games. The second half of my career, though, I was tossed 15 times. I'm not sure what to make of that other than, as I matured and became a team leader, I felt more responsibility. And that's what team leaders do: they defend their teams and themselves. A few of those times, there was a sense of frustration among our team, and I was just kind of taking a stand on behalf of everyone. Other times I just lost my temper over a couple of close calls and showed my frustration on the field. Sometimes you make mistakes. And obviously, I was a very intense player. I loved to win every day. So, sometimes when I couldn't get the job done, I'd get mad. I thought, *I know I can be better than what I'm showing.*

There were never any harsh feelings toward the umpires on my end, though. There's a special bond between the catcher and the home-plate umpire, and I took that very seriously. I started having conversations with the umpires when I reached professional baseball. I started doing it a lot in spring training the year they sent me to play in Double A Tulsa in 1991. I was already in big league camp and I wanted the umpires to know me a little bit since I was one of the top prospects in the organization at the time and I knew that I was very close to getting to the big leagues. During the games I played in, I made sure to say hello and introduce myself to the umpires just to start the relationship. In Double A I did that every day because the Double A umpires are also prospects who will soon make the big leagues just like the players there. Then when they called me up, I kept doing the same thing. I was communicating with the umpires, asking questions about close pitches and making sure I talked to them the right way.

If you've seen highlights of me catching and I turn a little bit to the right, it was because I was asking something to the home-plate umpire. That's how I communicated with the umpires. I didn't want to look him in the eye because that's disrespectful. I also made sure I spoke to him in a low voice, so sometimes not even the batter knew that I was talking to the umpire. He and I would discuss the pitch, or sometimes I let him know what I was going to call on the next pitch so he could have a better angle to see it. Especially on the inside part of the plate. On the inside pitches, whether from right-handers or left-handers, I made sure the umpire knew that I was coming in. Or I might tap him on his shin guards, which meant I was going one way, so he could come back a little more. That way he could see me from the best possible angle.

Nobody ever taught me that. I just figured it out on my own.

I think I had a pretty good relationship with most umpires. I had a couple of issues over the years, but that is all part of the game. I think if you ask home-plate umpires from the past or even from today about me, they would probably say that I was one of the best catchers for them to work with because I always wanted to be as quiet or calm as possible and move as little as possible so they could see the pitches. For example, if you're a home-plate umpire and I'm in front of you, I'll tell you that I'm going to call for a fastball in, but it's going to be a sinking fastball, so be ready. Be in a good spot to see that sinker. What umpire wouldn't like that, right? That makes your job easier. And that helps them to anticipate the pitch, which is going to make them a better umpire. I did that my whole career.

• • •

There was no way of knowing this at the time, but the 2007 campaign was kind of the beginning of the end. That was my last year making the All-Star team and also the last time I won a Gold Glove. My 2007 Gold Glove was my 13th. I was 35 years old, and, of course, as an athlete you're stubborn and focused on the moment. You are not thinking, *My skills aren't what they once were.* I was always in the moment, thinking about the next pitch call, next at-bat, next game, or next workout.

We went 88–74, which came up just shy of earning a postseason berth. Magglio went nuts with maybe the best hitting season I ever witnessed firsthand, and I saw some good ones. He batted .363 with 139 RBIs. We traded for Gary Sheffield in the offseason, and he did his thing, belting 25 home runs at 38 years old.

Sheff is one of those guys like Will Clark. We are good friends. I tended to get along well with guys like that because I wasn't afraid or intimidated to talk with them. In the couple of years we played together, Gary was always a teammate who told you straight-up what he liked and what he didn't like. He spoke up when he didn't like something, and we sat down and talked it out. There were things that happened during the season or during the game like a pitching change or something that he may have disagreed with.

Some of his comments could be very tough and hard on others, but you also had to understand him. It was nothing personal. Gary could be yelling at you one day and best friends the next. He was intense and a heck of a hitter. I think we really would have enjoyed playing together longer, especially earlier in our careers. There could have been some fireworks, but at the end of the day, we were going to shake hands and be friends.

The highlight of that 2007 season came on June 12 when Justin Verlander threw a no-hitter against the Milwaukee Brewers at Comerica Park. This certainly wasn't a surprise, at least in terms of any no-hitter being a surprise. His stuff was unhittable a lot of nights, but the other teams just had a few lucky hits. He was throwing hard that night like always—99 to 100 miles per hour—but to throw a no-hitter, you have to locate your pitches to different parts of the plate so the hitter isn't fixated on one particular spot. And he did that against the Brewers. He was moving it around everywhere, inside and outside corners. Justin also located the fastball in and out and up and in. We mixed it up a lot, too. He didn't throw too many fastballs. It was mostly change-ups and breaking balls.

JUSTIN VERLANDER
TIGERS PITCHER
"We didn't talk too much during the no-hitter, but we were very much on the same page. I think that in most great games you find the pitcher and the catcher are in a good rhythm, and this was no different. What I really remember was the end of it when he came running out to the mound. It was a fly ball, so I was looking out to right field. As soon as Magglio Ordonez caught it, I turned back around, and Pudge was right there in front of me, jumping up and down in my arms and giving me a big hug. It was really cool to be that young and have somebody older that excited. It was pretty special to me. To have a Hall of Fame catcher be that excited, it made me even more excited than I already was.

"It's a tradition after a no-hitter for the pitcher to get a gift for his catcher. And here I was in my second full year in the league, and there he was that far along in his career. I racked my brain thinking, 'What the hell do I get a guy like Pudge?' I just couldn't think of anything. A lot of guys get a nice watch for their catcher, but I thought he probably had every watch he ever wanted. I didn't have a ton of money either, so I couldn't buy him the type of watch he would want anyway.

"So I blew up the picture of him and I jumping into each other's arms after the final out, had it framed, and wrote a nice note on it thanking him for all his hard work. That's what I thought was special about it because I couldn't have done it without him. He was a great inspiration to me even as a pitcher. Back then when the catcher came out to visit the mound, I thought, 'Come on.' But I look back now and completely understand what he was doing and appreciate it more."

As I told the media after the game, "When you catch a no-hitter, it's like hitting 6-for-6. I didn't care what I did in my four at-bats today. I was just there to go out behind the plate and call a good game. That's one of the things that I take a lot of pride in. That's the beauty of this game. You never know when things like this are going to happen, and when they do happen, you've gotta enjoy it."

There was another highlight that season, as I became the first catcher to reach 500 career doubles, doing so against the Chicago White Sox on September 5. I finished the season batting .281 with 11 home runs, my fewest dingers since 1993.

A few days after the season ended, Dave Dombrowski called to inform me the team would be picking up the option on my deal, which was worth $13 million. They could have bought the last year out for $3 million, and I was obviously thrilled they didn't. Not only financially speaking, but I also loved playing for Jim Leyland and was quite comfortable in Detroit. The team's owner, Mike Ilitch, who I had a great relationship with, said in an interview a few days before Dave called, "Pudge did a big thing for us, putting a face on the franchise. He's made a lot of contributions."

That meant a lot to me. Mike was one of my favorite owners I ever played for, and I was saddened to hear of his passing early in 2017. I was hopeful he could be there for my Hall of Fame induction. Those nearly five years in Detroit were such a significant chapter of my career, especially when no one else was really willing to take a chance on me with a long-term deal.

Yes, nearly five years. I came up two months shy. We were a few days away from the July 31 trade deadline in 2008 and not having the kind of season everyone expected from us. We were just a few games above .500. During the offseason we had traded for my former teammate with the Marlins, Miggy Cabrera, and were the favorite to win the division. It just didn't come together.

I was hitting the ball well, nearly at .300, and really all of my offensive numbers were improved from the season before. Jim called me in his office and told me that the team was going to give more playing time to Brandon Inge, whose contract they had extended a few years during the offseason. This meant I wouldn't be playing every day. Brandon was younger and making a lot of money with a multi-year contract and he was disappointed that he hadn't been an everyday starter. He also said that he didn't want to catch, that he wanted to play third base, but we had Carlos Guillen at third base at the time. Miggy could play there, too.

I did have a no-trade clause, but my goal first and foremost always was to be playing every day. I had no idea if a trade was possible or if they were even talking to anyone. I did talk with Dave and mentioned that the New York Yankees needed a catcher since Jorge Posada was recently lost for the season with an injury. See, watching ESPN every night helped me in multiple ways.

We were in Cleveland the last week of July, and Dave and Jim called me in when I arrived at the park. I was completely surprised to learn that I had been traded to New York for relief pitcher Kyle Farnsworth. Also, I had never been traded before, so it was a new feeling. They said, "Look, we need to talk to you. We have you included in a potential trade to the Yankees because Jorge Posada got hurt, and they really, really want you there."

I was having a great year, and the Yankees were in third place, four games out of first. When that happened I started thinking about going to New York, but at the same time I was thinking, *I love Detroit, I love being here, and I have a no-trade clause.* So, I told them to give me some more time to think it over. I called my agent, Scott Boras, and he told me, "Look, go to the Yankees because, no matter what, the Tigers want to give Brandon Inge an opportunity to play more. If you stay there, they're going to play both you and Brandon, and I prefer you to continue to play every day."

The next day I told the Tigers, "Okay, I'm going."

Saying goodbye to my teammates was tough. Saying goodbye to Jim was even tougher. We are both emotional guys. We had a long hug in his office, and I think we both were fighting back a tear or two. I loved playing for him so much. He patted me on the back and wished me all the best, and I was off to New York. It was time to move on, time to join the pinstripes. And I was beyond excited because I was getting a chance to play in the Big Apple, a chance to play alongside Derek Jeter and my former Rangers teammate Alex Rodriguez. This was going to be fun.

Or not.

When I got to the Yankees, I was expecting to play every day because that's what they brought me in for. And then there were a couple starting pitchers—again, I don't want to name names, but you can look it up—who wanted to continue working with the catcher that they felt comfortable with, and that was Jose Molina. So, I ended up playing two or three days out of the week instead of playing every day and I just was never able to find a groove offensively that way. I am a creature of habit, so I needed to be playing every day to perform at my best. There's no routine when you are coming to the park with no idea if you are playing or not.

Those pitchers wanted the backup to catch for them. That was a little disappointing because I was just there to help the team. I was just there to learn the pitching staff as quickly as I could. And I studied very hard to get the best information I could from the starting pitchers. That was the first time in my career that some pitchers preferred other catchers. I didn't understand it. I mean, I was kind of like, "Give me the chance to work with you. I'm sure you're going to like what I do for you, too." But that never happened since they wanted to continue with their routine.

The entire New York experience went much differently than I was anticipating and it probably was the greatest disappointment of my career. When the trade happened, I expected to stay in New York for a long time. They were thinking about moving Posada from catcher to first base, so the plan was to bring me in and have me there for a few years. But Jorge decided to come back and catch the following year, which is understandable. You know, he's the catcher for the Yankees. I didn't get mad at what he did because that's part of baseball. I found out in the offseason, but I didn't get upset or anything. It's already done. I spent a great few months there in New York, and I think I did a pretty good job with the opportunity I got there.

What I was disappointed about was that I was expecting to come back to the Yankees again the following year and be the main catcher on the team. You know, it would have been nice to finish my career with the Yankees like a lot of players love to do.

It's hard for me to explain how surprising a trade is when it's never happened before. Yes, I was open to it, but the mentality of a ballplayer is: wherever you are you expect to stay there. A few days before Jim called me into his office, I was thinking I would retire with Detroit, that I would play there until I couldn't play anymore. That was 100 percent my mind-set, especially because of my relationship with Dave and Jim and with Mike and his family. They wanted to go with Brandon, a guy they drafted and developed, which was perfectly their right.

Then, as a player, I had to tell myself, *Okay, now it's not going to be the Tigers anymore.* That was tough because I played five great years there. But when I went to the Yankees, I opened up my mind and said, *Okay, now I would love to wear these pinstripes until I retire from baseball.* Just to be in New York and be recognized as another Yankee who plays four or five years there would have been great. That was my thinking at the end of the 2008 season, and trust me: I was telling Scott Boras that over and over and over. "I want to stay with the Yankees. Try to get a deal done."

That was until Jorge decided he wanted to remain a catcher. If he had followed through with the plan of moving to first base, I would have probably been a Yankee the rest of my career. Again, if there was anyone in the world who understands wanting to remain a catcher despite being 37, 38, it was me. I completely respect that. I know how that works. There were conversations here and there over my career about changing positions, but I'd really never paid attention to it. I think they would talk with my agent about that stuff. I was going to finish my career at one position, and that's why I worked so hard throughout my career. I was a catcher. Once a catcher, always a catcher, that's the way I look at it. And Jorge, who is also from Puerto Rico, had a few more really nice years before finishing up at first base. It was really a great career for him with 275 home runs and four World Series. I guess Puerto Rico knows how to produce catchers, huh?

During my time with the Yankees, it wasn't that difficult for me to catch Mariano Rivera's legendary cut fastball. Because it's only one pitch—a cutter. The only thing Mariano wanted was the cutter, so I just had to put the catcher's glove down low or up high. Those were his two locations. It's almost like two different pitches, low and high. He was a killer throwing fastballs up and in to lefties. It was almost impossible for a left-hander to hit that pitch. Even if the batter made contact, the head of his bat would probably land in right field. I actually had a couple of hits off him, including a home run in Arlington back in 2000. But again, the pitcher always has the advantage. As a pitcher you get more outs than all the hits I get against you.

Every big leaguer wants to experience what it's like to play in New York, and it doesn't disappoint. I was honored to play in the pinstripes even if it was a much shorter time than anyone anticipated. And we fell just short of the playoffs at 89–73.

With Jorge returning behind the plate, the Yankees didn't need me. I was going to be 37 for the 2009 season, but I felt great.

I played some winter ball and I was proud and thrilled beyond words to be representing Puerto Rico that March in the World Baseball Classic. Our pool games took place at Hiram Bithorn Stadium in San Juan, where I played so many games as a teenager. We won our pool, too, and I was hitting the ball as well as ever, batting .500 for the tournament.

There was just one problem. When the tournament began, which was in the midst of spring training, I was still a free agent. I had a few offers, but I wanted to make sure it was a situation where I would at least have the opportunity to play every day. I think my performance for Puerto Rico showed everyone that I wasn't quite done yet.

12

A Return to the
Lone Star State

WHEN I WAS CATCHING, I WOULD INDICATE TO THE FIRST BASEMAN or third baseman that I was calling for a pitch inside. I just looked at them. And by that point the pitcher is already committed to throw, so there's no way the coaches are telling the batters anything. That's when I would look and move my hand, give a quick signal, or just nod my head or bend it to the left or right, so they move one step toward the line. The infielders always paid attention to me.

I would decide which pitch to call by looking at the batter all the time. I'd see where his feet were and could sometimes tell what he was looking for. Sometimes I would even call the pitch that he wants. If he's sitting back in the box, I might call for the fastball because he wants more space to be in front. I'd call for the fastball because he was looking for it, and sometimes when a hitter looks for a fastball, he overswings. And when you overswing, it's a fly ball or an easy ground ball.

Whether I talked to the batters or not all depended on the situation. Early on, when the game started, I would say hello, ask him how he is doing, wish him luck, tell him to have a great game, and that's about it. I wasn't a trash talker behind the plate because I didn't want other catchers to do that to me. To me Major League Baseball means something. And if you're doing those kinds of things, you're disrespecting the game. You're disrespecting the uniform that you wear, the team you're playing against, and the fans. You don't want to play that way.

That's the way the older players taught me when I came up in 1991. On the team the Texas Rangers had when I got called up, we had plenty of guys who had some big league experience. So, I learned from Day One. We had five veteran starting pitchers who didn't joke around, and the pitchers in the bullpen didn't joke around. All the position players, too, especially in the middle of the diamond, were very serious. I could see Julio Franco out there at second base, Gary Pettis in center field, veteran guys like that. Everywhere you looked, there were big names, veteran players who commanded respect, and I learned how to respect the game from them really quick.

Too prepare myself, I'd take a scouting report from the night before and read from the leadoff batter through the nine hole. Then when we arrived at the park the next day, I'd look at particulars while watching video and see if that matched the report. I'd also add my own notes, then do some work on possible pinch-hitters, some of whom might even start since we didn't have the opposing team's lineup at that point. We usually had that about three hours before the first pitch. The first time through the lineup, I'm calling pitches based just on my reports—what the pitcher and I talked about beforehand. By the second time through, however, I'm calling what I've seen myself during that first at-bat, and then that's going to be my basis for the remainder of the game. Obviously, by the fourth at-bat, the scouting report doesn't mean much if the guy has struck out three times on the same breaking stuff.

With power hitters I always pitched them inside all the time, so that they couldn't extend their arms. That's what they are looking to do so they can elevate the ball. So, we wanted to keep their hands close to their body by throwing curveballs and sliders away. When we threw fastballs, they were only inside or perhaps outside and low. That was the only exception, especially if I knew the hitter was prone to chasing. But my favorite combination— my one-two punch for power hitters—was to start with a slider down and away, and if they fouled it off, I'd come back with a fastball in. That almost never failed.

There might be nothing more important in calling pitches as changing the eye level on the hitter. I had 12 different positions for where I would set up and I would move around not only left to right but higher and lower as well. My entire focus would be on those 12 location spots. I'd even move my arm in and out based on where I crouched. I'd practice just moving around to the different targets, going through all 12 and throwing down to second on each position since there would be different release points on each throw.

Even in my dreams today, I am playing baseball. And never batting. I'm always behind the plate. Most players looked forward to their at-bats. Not me. I just wanted to be behind the plate, calling pitches, working with my pitcher. As far as hitting, I never really tried to use my catching knowledge at the plate. I just saw the ball and hit it. You can ask my former hitting coach Rudy Jaramillo, who taught me so much. He always said, "Pudge never thinks about pitches. He just thinks about being on time with his swing." I love that man. He taught me how to hit.

And Rudy always focused on 60/40. That means 60 percent of the weight is on the back leg and 40 percent on the front. It helps to stay back and be on time. I tried to land early, stay inside, and throw the hands. If you threw me a breaking ball or a fastball or a change-up or a splitter, whatever it was, I always tried to think about 60/40 and staying on time. It was very rare that I pulled the ball to left field in batting practice. Every ball that I hit in BP was from second base to right field. And that was the approach that I took to the game: stay back. Home runs come on their own. If I looked for home runs, I would have batted about .190. You know what a home run is? It's a perfect swing.

Obviously, the fastball is everybody's favorite pitch to hit because when a pitcher has a good breaking ball it's almost impossible to hit. If a batter hits a slider 450 feet for a home run, I'm calling for that pitch again because he's not thinking about it. He thinks that the pitcher is not going to throw it again since he hit it a mile the last time up. On the fastball inside, when guys turn on it and hit it 500 feet foul, I call for that pitch again. And it's a 99 percent chance that batter is going to be sitting on another pitch, and the head of the bat is going to be over first or third base. Or it's going to be a foul tip off his foot or a long foul ball again. The hitter thinks, *Okay, I've got him. He's not going to throw me that pitch again.* Bullshit. That's right where you need to go now.

Of course, there's a lot of stealing signs in baseball—whether it's what the catcher is calling or it's the third-base coach or manager calling for a bunt or a steal. Personally, I never stole signs. It just wasn't my thing. Also I was an instinctive hitter, so knowing the pitch wasn't really a huge advantage. I would sometimes just have a hunch what was going to be thrown, but that only happened on occasion. Some hitters would give anything to know the pitch, so they were always trying to gain any advantage in finding out. I just didn't like it because all it would do is take away from my focus, and my focus at the plate was: see the ball, hit the ball. Keep it simple.

Pitchers and catchers change signals a lot—sometimes twice in an inning, though that was rare. Obviously, no one is going to use the same signals an entire game. You might as well just walk over and hand the signs to the other team if that's the case. We went into every game with four groups of signs we could fall back on if needed, depending on the situation. If the batter starts taking too many close pitches for balls, that's when you have to go talk with the pitcher and change the signs. Maybe a disciplined hitter lays off a close pitch here or there, or they just get lucky—but not consistently. Maybe Ted Williams and Barry Bonds. That's about it. If it's anyone else, I think they probably would be stealing signs.

Know what else we did sometimes? If there was a guy on second base, obviously stealing signs or trying to, I'd go out to the mound and call the next three or four pitches. No signs. Then there's nothing they could do. Slider, fastball, change-up, and if they put one into play, maybe I'd walk out real quick and call three more.

Something else we would often do with a runner on second base would be to change the indicator. Say the indicator is two fingers, so I start with four, then put down two, which tells the pitcher the next signal is the pitch. Let's say I put down a fist for a change-up, then I put one finger down and pat the inside of my thigh, maybe the hitter thinks inside fastball.

The strategy of it is twofold. While you are trying to make it as difficult as possible for the runner to steal a sign, you want to keep it simple for your pitcher. That way they can focus on throwing strikes, hitting their location, and using proper mechanics rather than having to figure out what the catcher is calling. The last thing you want to do is create confusion for the pitcher. They have enough on their mind to begin with.

As a catcher, it's important to treat each pitcher differently. Some liked quick and simple signs, so maybe the second signal is the go-to for however long they are in the game. Some were more concerned than others about the signs possibly being stolen by the other team, so they want to change it up more. Some worked quickly, some worked slow, some threw over to first more, wanting to make sure the base runners don't run. Some had no clue how to hold a runner, which, of course, made my job more difficult.

• • •

I guess you could call it a backhanded compliment, not that anyone meant any disrespect in the least. But more and more, teammates and opposing players were telling me how they watched me when they were growing up. Or that I was one of their favorites when they were younger. Or that they had a poster of me in their bedroom. Again, it was an honor to hear that from any fan, never mind a peer. It was just, well, I was still playing, and it made me feel old.

I really had come full circle. For several years when I came up with the Texas Rangers, I was the youngest guy on the team. It wasn't until Derek Jeter in 1996, my sixth season, that an American League Rookie of the Year was younger than I was. I was the youngest guy in Major League Baseball for each of my first two seasons. And now, entering the 2009 campaign, I was one of the oldest at 37. Yet I was still playing the most physically demanding position. Yes, I was probably stubborn, but my father's words never left my mind. "Ivan," he said, "you were born to be a catcher." And I was going out as one.

While we were playing the World Baseball Classic, which I think is a fantastic event, I signed with the Houston Astros. That was March, which is late in spring training really. That was kind of by design, though, to see what opportunities were out there. Plus, I was never a big fan of spring training anyhow. After my rookie year, I arrived late throughout my career. I was playing winter ball every year, so I didn't need six or seven weeks of spring training. That's one of those baseball traditions that really no longer make sense. Spring training was instituted back in the day for players, who had to work regular jobs in the offseason, to work their way back into shape. Baseball is a year-round job for us, and it has been long before I even started playing. We are always in shape.

One of my teammates with the Astros was Hunter Pence, an always-hustling outfielder who grew up in Arlington and told me I was his favorite player when he was younger. As I was saying, this was becoming the norm rather than the rarity.

Playing most of the 2009 season with Houston was challenging. I had no problem with the fans, the city, or the organization. It was just, like with the New York Yankees the year before, I wasn't playing regularly. I'd play three times a week or even less sometimes. I wanted to perform at the level I was capable of and I was still giving the best I had when I was out there, but I needed to play more. I'd start to get going with the bat, then sit a few days, and it was a downhill spiral.

I never went to talk with a manager or general manager about playing time. I was always professional. That's how I was raised and that's how I was taught to respect the game by my teammates with the Rangers when I first came up. That one year in Houston, though, I did talk with manager Cecil Cooper a few times—but not to show my displeasure. I just told him, "Hey, I totally understand the future is coming up, the future you guys are hoping for. Those younger catchers are ready now, and you want to see them. I get it." That strategy made sense, especially because we weren't winning, as the Astros finished 74–88 that season. If we were winning or in the playoff race, I think I would have played more. I was still solid defensively—at least I'd like to think I was. I was still throwing guys out on the base paths and I still had a little pop in my bat. I just had to rely on what I had learned. That meant knowing what is going to happen in any situation or any pitch, whether hitting, blocking, throwing, or calling the game.

There were some milestones that occurred during my five months with Houston, and the first came against the Chicago

Cubs on May 17. Yes, at historic Wrigley Field, I took Rich Harden deep for my 300th career home run. I was never a power hitter. I hit a home run about every 33 plate appearances over my career, which comes out to less than 15 per season. I just played for a long time. Mike Piazza, Johnny Bench, Carlton Fisk, and Yogi Berra were all catchers who had more power than I did.

I was very happy when Piazza was voted into the Hall of Fame in 2016, a year before me. I had great respect for him. He was arguably the best hitting catcher to ever take the field and he called a heck of a game. Mike was a much better catcher than he was sometimes given credit for.

Another milestone, the one I am most proud of, came on June 17, 2009, when I caught my 2,227th game. That broke the all-time mark held by another Pudge, Carlton Fisk. Even better, the game was in Arlington against the Rangers. The fans gave me several standing ovations, and that meant so much to me. Honestly, it felt like a home game.

Fittingly, the game went extra innings, too, and I caught every pitch. There is nothing more important in life, and sports, than showing up. That was my main objective, taking the field and being there for my teammates. My former manager, the great Johnny Oates, would always promise me the day off after I played a bunch of straight games. More times than not, though, when he sat down the following day to write out the lineup, he would write my name down and later apologize to me. Know what, though? I never minded because it was an honor that he thought that much of me. I didn't want a day off.

On August 18 of that season, I was traded back to the Rangers. This was an unexpected joy to return to my team, my organization. I never wanted to leave. I was overcome with great happiness at being able to come back one more time. The trade happened really quickly, like within a few hours of the first phone call. I left everything in Houston. I just took my baseball bag and drove the four hours from Houston to Arlington. I wanted to play that night but couldn't quite make it in time. I arrived at the park around 6:00. I just wanted to take the field with the Rangers again. I drove a little faster than I should have.

The team's captain at the time and one of my favorite guys in baseball, Michael Young, told the media, "It's huge for our fanbase. He might be the best player in the history of our organization and probably the most popular. This is just a great move on all fronts."

That six-week stretch was so much fun. The team was on the cusp of winning back-to-back league titles and ended up winning 87 games that season. I was supposed to be the backup, but I ended up playing more often than not. I got into 28 games and had more than 100 at-bats down the stretch.

My first game back was in Arlington. In a nice gesture, slick-hitting outfielder David Murphy gave up his No. 7, so I could wear it again. How cool was that? That meant so much to me, being back home and wearing my old number. The fans gave me a standing ovation for that first at-bat, and I had a good day with three hits, including a double.

At season's end the question was, "What's next?" I still felt good and I wanted to play, so it was just a matter of finding the right fit. I played 121 games during the 2009 season, had nearly 450 plate appearances, and yes, like in the past, wanted to play. I was all for teaching and mentoring younger catchers, which was fun, but I didn't want to be sitting on the bench.

There was one last stop for me on what would be an incredible 23 years in professional baseball.

Retirement

IT WOULD HAVE BEEN FITTING TO FINISH MY CAREER WITH THE Texas Rangers, and they offered me arbitration before the free agency period even began. That meant we could figure out how much I would be paid at a later date, but I would play the 2010 season with them. The only downside to that was they wanted me to be the backup. As it turned out, they actually used five catchers that season, so there really wasn't a starter, but that's in hindsight. As always, I wanted to play.

Look, there are very few players who are fortunate enough to still be playing in the big leagues at 38 years old, never mind as a catcher. I was incredibly lucky to have been healthy enough to play that long. Here's a promise, though: anyone who has had their name written onto that lineup card the majority of their career doesn't want to sit. I was the same way. So, although I would have loved to spend my last few years with the Rangers, I felt like I could still start. And my agent, Scott Boras, felt the same way. So, we decided to play the market.

We had several one-year offers, which would have been okay, but I really wanted to sign a two-year deal and then see how I felt after that. Another problem was that a lot of teams thought I was going to be content being a backup while I fully expected to start. That was a talking point for sure.

The Washington Nationals stepped up with a really strong offer: two years, $6 million. That was more than a lot of people thought I'd get, so I was pretty happy. Also, they said I was going to be the starter. I know a lot of older players learn to become backups, but that just wasn't going to work for me. I needed to play. That was my oxygen.

The first year with the Nationals, I played a lot of games, though it was tough being at the bottom of the lineup. That was different, and I didn't enjoy it because there were a lot fewer guys on base than I was used to. I played in 111 games despite a two-week stint on the disabled list. My numbers were decent, as I batted .266 with 49 RBIs. And I stole two bases—how's that for an old catcher? I finished my career with 127 steals, and only a handful of catchers have more. My best season by far was in 1999 when I was named MVP. I stole 25 that season and I stole 10 bases on three other occasions, the last being in 2008 when I was 36. I went 10-for-11 that year.

We finished that 2010 season at 69–93, which was actually 10 more wins than the team had the year before. The highlight of the season was catching Stephen Strasburg, who was born exactly one week before I signed with the Rangers. Imagine being able to catch Nolan Ryan at the beginning of my career and this kid at the end. That's pretty amazing.

I was on the disabled list with a bad back, but I wanted to catch his first game. And I know he wanted me to catch it. That meant a lot to both of us. They had me take batting practice before they activated me for that night's game against the Pittsburgh Pirates. I also had to review the scouting reports, which I did without Stephen. We decided he had enough going on, so he should enjoy it and just focus on his pitching. He would be reviewing reports the rest of his career. For this one night, I'd handle all that for him.

We were sitting there in the dugout before taking the field and I told him, "Let's start this leadoff hitter off with a breaking ball."

He said, "Nah, let's go fastball."

But he trusted me for the most part that night, and we had so much fun. Stephen pitched seven innings and struck out 14. We won the game 5–2. The stadium was electric and sold out, which wasn't always the case.

The kid was filthy that night. And he was really respectful toward me, which I appreciated. We worked really well together the remainder of the season. When the press asked me about him after the game, I told them, "I've been catching a lot of guys, but this kid is unbelievable. The most amazing thing is he's around the plate, he throws strikes, and he's always in the strike zone. Normally, especially guys that young, like Stephen, they come and get behind in the count, but he didn't do that today. He just attacked the strike zone."

Stephen finished that season with 92 strikeouts in 68 innings, which is ridiculous. That's like me in Little League. I'm just glad I was behind the plate when he pitched and not in the batter's box.

Later in the season the Nationals called up their catching prospect, Wilson Ramos. I knew he would be my replacement and I worked with him as much as I could. Not only just about catching mechanics either. I preached to him the importance of being a good leader of the pitching staff and being a leader in general. It's important for the catcher to be in control during the game.

I enjoyed working with the younger players. I spent a ton of time with Ian Desmond, who has really become a fantastic player. But since Wilson and I were both catchers, most of my time was with him. Our manager, Jim Riggleman, talked to me in 2011 about the fact that Wilson was going to play more and more. They still let me start Opening Day, which was nice. I know Jim was dreading the conversation, but I thought it went well. Afterward, Jim told the press, "It was one of the best conversations I've ever had with a ballplayer since I've been managing. He was just first class, and it really speaks to the quality individual that he is."

Look, I had no problem. I was a grown man and I knew that Wilson was a great player. I just wanted to help the team win. I had won an MVP award and won the World Series, so I knew how to succeed. When Jim and I sat down and talked, he saw me for the person that I was.

I felt like there was a lot of baseball left in me. I was playing for a great organization, in a great city, and in a beautiful ballpark. You appreciate that more when the end is close. You think about maybe another postseason, maybe 3,000 hits.

But it was good for both Wilson and me. We got along well, and I was with him all the time. I was still in great shape. I was working my ass off, I wanted to help, and I wanted to play well when I was given the chance. I taught him everything I could. We would sit down and talk a lot, kind of like a player/coach relationship. The general managers and front offices are always thinking about the future. They are thinking about developing the younger guys, and that's how it works. I was a young guy once, too.

That last year, though, I realized something had changed. I was playing just once or twice a week, which was beyond hard on me. Sitting on the bench, not being a part of the action. Honestly, many days I just felt like a coach, like there was no need for me to bring my gear. I was just a bystander.

And, I mean, I'm not an idiot. I'm not one of those guys who thought I was the same player as I was in my prime. I was batting around .220 with little power. The game was really getting more difficult for me. I was struggling, and my body couldn't do the things it could just a few years earlier. I, though, could still throw. I threw out 52 percent of base stealers, and the league average was 28 percent. I was really proud of that.

That was a really frustrating year. I guess reality was slowly finding its way to my brain. It was time. I had a feeling it was going to be my last season. Now, it's easy to retire in October or December. That's why so many players retire, or say they are retiring, and then come back. I didn't want to be like one of those guys or like those boxers who used to retire after every fight. Of course, they want to retire when they are exhausted and in pain, thinking of going through that all over again.

Who knows how many times I changed my mind that offseason. Countless. I didn't really want to end my career. I mean, I guess no one wants to stop doing the thing they love most in this world. But mentally, I was not ready for another spring training and another year of sitting on the bench. There was some interest, and a few clubs offered guaranteed contracts, but the passion wasn't in me anymore. It was time. I also didn't want to be the guy who didn't know when to leave. I didn't want to play at a level so far below my peak years.

During that winter one day, I felt like I was ready to retire. And then the next day, I wasn't so sure. This went back and forth during the offseason. I even played winter ball. In the end, though, after talking it over with my family and friends, it was time, and I needed to accept it. It's part of being a professional athlete.

My wife, Patricia, and I talked for many, many hours during those months. She was my sounding board. She listened to all my reasons for trying to play another year. She listened to all my reasons for retiring. In the end she was the one to convince me it was time to say farewell. The night before I made my final decision, Patricia told me, "You have already played so much baseball. And now you can go out the big door on the grandest stage. You don't want to wait and be run out of the game. That would be beneath you."

I try and not have regrets in my life and I am quite proud of my career. I guess if there was one regret on an individual level it's not having 3,000 hits. I was 156 hits shy of 3,000. I still think about it today. If you think about it, 156 isn't a huge number. And over the course of 21 seasons, that's not many. That's what is so great about baseball, though. We cherish its history and these magical numbers, and, you know, for a catcher who never changed positions (I was almost never the designated hitter with only 53 starts there in my career), I think 2,844 is plenty. And it's a record for the position. Only two other catchers had 2,000, Jason Kendall and Carlton Fisk. That's just for games in which they played catcher, of course, not overall.

But 2,844 is a lot of hits. I hit the ball a lot to where nobody could catch it, which is the goal of this great game of baseball. Three hits in 10 at-bats is a .300 average, which is good, but you're still making an out seven out of 10 times. It's not easy. It's not an easy game to play, especially when that ball is coming toward you at over 90 miles per hour with movement to different parts of the strike zone.

I was never really into my statistics. My father and I always had arguments about this. He would tell me what my numbers were, what I was batting, and I just didn't care. My goal was staying in the moment. My dad, bless his heart, would just keeping yelling at me about all these numbers, and I'd yell back, "Papi, I don't care."

It wasn't only him either. Fans, teammates, even Patricia, they were always telling me how many home runs I had or how many

Here I am as an anxious rookie during my debut season with the Rangers in 1991.
(*AP Images*)

Left: I hug Kenny Rogers and Will Clark after Rogers throws a perfect game on July 28, 1994. (*AP Images*)

Below: I celebrate scoring off a Will Clark double with Juan Gonzalez. It's amazing that two guys from the same Puerto Rican town ended up starting on the same major league team. (*AP Images*)

During my long career, I threw out would-be base stealers at a 46 percent rate and led the league in that category nine times. (*AP Images*)

I hit a double against the Chicago White Sox in 1999. As part of my MVP season, I hit .332 with 35 home runs and 113 RBIs that year.
(*AP Images*)

Johnny Bench, my idol, and I are the only two catchers with at least 10 Gold Gloves.
(*AP Images*)

Here I am during the 2000 season, when I hit a career-best .347. *(AP Images)*

Florida Marlins president David Samson (left) and general manager Larry Beinfest (right) announce my signing in 2003. (*AP Images*)

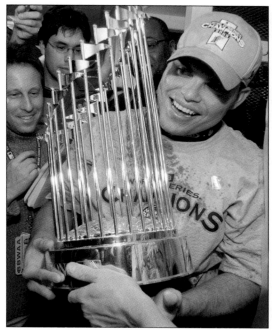

I celebrate with the World Series trophy after helping the Florida Marlins defeat the New York Yankees in 2003. (*AP Images*)

I carry my daughter, Amanda, on my shoulders after defeating the New York Yankees in Game 6 of the World Series. (*AP Images*)

I smile after signing a four-year deal with the Detroit Tigers in 2004. *(AP Images)*

Left: I pose before my first of five seasons with the Detroit Tigers. I enjoyed playing a role in helping turn around that storied franchise. *(AP Images)*

Above: I hang out with my son, Dereck, who is now a professional baseball player as well, and my dad, Jose. *(Ivan Rodriguez Family)*

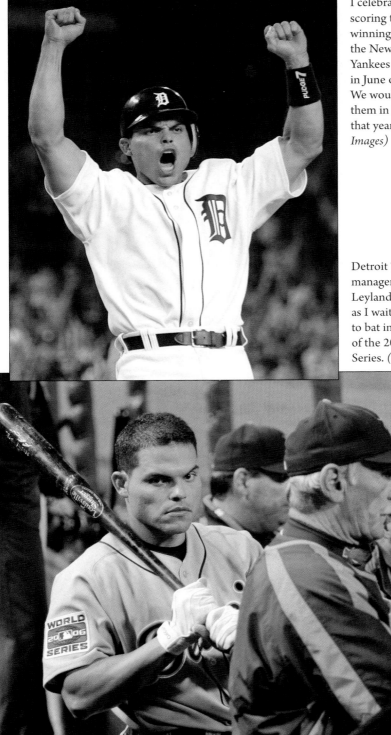

I celebrate after scoring the game-winning run against the New York Yankees in a game in June of 2006. We would also face them in the ALDS that year. *(AP Images)*

Detroit Tigers manager Jim Leyland looks on as I wait my turn to bat in Game 4 of the 2006 World Series. *(AP Images)*

My family stands alongside me during an emotional ceremony in 2012 to announce my retirement from baseball. *(AP Images)*

Nolan Ryan congratulates me on my induction into the Rangers Hall of Fame in 2013. *(AP Images)*

RBIs I needed to break a record, and it was nice to hear, I was always humbled they knew and cared, but it just wasn't why I was playing. Patricia would read that I became the first catcher to do this or that, and she would tell me all excited, and I would smile. If that made her happy, I was happy.

I made the official announcement of my retirement on April 24, 2012. I was no longer a big league baseball player. That's all I had known since I was a teenager. I wanted to hold the press conference in Arlington, so I went to the ballpark there. Then they drove me on to the field in a convertible. The fans gave me a standing ovation, and I waved and smiled. I told them yes, I may not be in between the lines anymore, but I will always be there for my fans and for baseball.

That was a special moment for me, and I was saying thank you to those great fans in my own heart and mind. They always treated me well. The team's manager at the time, Ron Washington, said of me, "He was the best I've ever seen. He had the quickest release and accuracy I've ever seen. He was the scariest guy to have back there when you were at first base. He could beat up with the bat big time. He was a special catcher."

Of course, Nolan Ryan was there. He was the team president at the time. He told me then like he would always tell me when I was younger, "Do me a favor and keep busy when you retire. No one should be at home all the time. Don't be that guy on the sofa watching TV all day."

And Nolan was right about taking care of other business, developing another career, and focusing on it. I started playing a lot more golf, too. That's been my saving grace. I travel a lot for business, which is good for me, or I would just be watching baseball on TV all day waiting for someone to invite me to play golf.

That first year, though, that was tough. I'd even call it "brutal." There was no spring training, no April baseball, no Opening Day. I didn't even watch baseball that first season because it was too painful. I am pretty sure I drove my wife, Patricia, crazy. We had been married for five years at that point, and she was not used to having me around all the time, every day. Well, at least from March through September.

PATRICIA GOMEZ
WIFE

"The last two years of his career were very difficult because he wasn't given the opportunity to play every day, and he was accustomed to playing daily. I would tell him to take it easy because he had already played so much, plus he had to understand that they had to give an opportunity to the youngsters and have a veteran like him help them.

"The decision to retire wasn't easy. The game was his passion, and it was the only thing he'd done practically his entire life. I believe the first year of retirement was the most difficult. When spring training arrived, when the games started, he sat there staring ahead like he didn't know what to do with himself. It was sad and difficult, but slowly and surely, he started adjusting to his new business life and to the game of golf. That's his new passion, and because he's so disciplined, he doesn't mind playing alone. He takes his clubs whenever he travels. He goes to meetings and makes time to play golf. He also rides his bike and exercises, though not as often because of so many business trips that don't allow for much free time."

For the first few months there, I didn't do much of anything. I almost had to readjust back to civilian life. What did the rest of the world do during baseball season? The hell if I knew, I was always playing. Know what I thought of a lot during that time? I looked back on the baseball memories with my teammates and coaches. I watched some clips of me on YouTube—even me arguing with an umpire. That would always make me chuckle.

I would think about my first contract for $21,500. I was 16 years old. And then I was making like $800 a month in the minor leagues, maybe $1,000 in Double A. That's why we were living with six or seven players in the same apartment. Even that first year I was promoted to the Rangers, I made like $82,000 for the season. That was a nice raise after making $5,000 the year before, but it's not exactly like I could buy all these houses and cars.

In fact, the first thing I did that offseason, which would have been 1991, was go back to Puerto Rico and buy my parents a nice place to live. They worked so hard for my brother and me growing up. They weren't making much money, but I always had the baseball equipment I needed, and we always had food to eat.

Obviously, I made a lot of money in my career, more than $100 million. Well, that's before taxes and the agents. I don't think the money changed anything, though. Sure, I was living better, but that didn't change me as a person. And I don't think money should change people. I know it's needed, and everybody wants to make money, but I was still the same person. I bought a nice home and a boat, but I used all that stuff with my family. It was more for them to enjoy and make them happy than for me. I didn't show it off or bring my teammates down because I'm not a real showy person.

I remember when I called my father after I got called up to the majors. I said, "Papi, you don't have to work so hard anymore.

Our family doesn't have to worry day-to-day about having money to pay the bills. I'm a major league player and I can take care of the family."

That was a proud day for me. After I signed some of the bigger deals, I bought my mother and father new homes and my brother, too. I still send money to my parents every month, so they don't need to work and stress anymore. Both of my parents retired a long time ago, and I've been sending money for 15 years or so. I want them to be taken care of—like they took care of me.

So, while I was obviously depressed during those first few months of retirement, I would think about my parents and being able to help them and make their lives better. And I would think about that first contract and having no money in the minor leagues. I look back now and appreciate those times because they made me tougher as a person. It didn't all come easy for me.

And I would think about my family. In the end it's all about family for me—baseball and family.

14

All-Star Games

I LOVED THE ALL-STAR GAME. YES, IT WAS AN EXHIBITION, AND THE games didn't have the competitive feeling of a regular-season contest—even after they made that absurd rule about the winning league hosting the World Series. Come on, you're going to make an exhibition game have more meaning toward the World Series than the 162 games we play for six months? That made no sense to most of us, but I still loved going.

You know what I enjoyed the most about All-Star Games? It was being there and taking the family there since they always wanted to go. I remember being in the clubhouse with all the other players, sitting at a long table full of baseball helmets and a bunch of other stuff we had to sign. Then we would go out, and the media would be all over the place.

It was a great place to be in the summertime. I know that a lot of people want to be on the beach. They want to be surfing, having fun on the water. But for 20-some years of my career, I never spent a summer on the beach. And I didn't miss that at all. Not when I was busy with baseball and All-Star Games. Some players wanted to just take three days off and go on vacation—but not me.

I was named an All-Star 14 times and voted a starter 12 times, and every time was an incredible honor. It was a joy to play in the game. What was really cool was having the opportunity to hang out with some of the different guys and call them my teammates for a few days. And before interleague play, we never saw those National League guys, so that made it even cooler. Those were players you only got to see on television.

I was 20 years old when I made my first All-Star team in 1992, and the game was in San Diego at Jack Murphy Stadium. My son, Dereck, was my only child born at the time. My grandpa took him to the great zoo they had in San Diego while I was at the ballpark.

Looking back at the lineups, the rosters were really impressive. The National League had Ozzie Smith, Tony Gwynn, Barry Bonds, Ryne Sandberg, and Tom Glavine. All those guys are now in the Baseball Hall of Fame with the exception of Bonds, who damn well should be.

Our American League team was loaded, too, with Roberto Alomar, Ken Griffey Jr., Cal Ripken Jr., Paul Molitor, and Mark McGwire, who should also be in Cooperstown with the rest of them. That's what our world is all about. When you work hard, you're going to get there.

The following year was the All-Star Game everyone talks about to this day, when Randy Johnson threw his blazing fastball over the head of John Kruk. I believe it was going 98 miles per hour, but it was still rising, so it looked like it was going 198 miles per hour. I didn't know Randy was going to do that before the inning started, but I could tell how nervous Kruk was coming to the plate. He was already sweating, so I told him, "Let's have some fun."

He wasn't having any fun, though. That poor guy wanted nothing to do with Randy. Honestly, none of us wanted to face Randy, especially left-handed batters, and Kruk had never faced him before. It was meant to be funny, and I think it worked out like that. At least for everyone beside poor Kruk. After Randy threw it way over Kruk's head, he exhaled deeply. I gave him a pat on the helmet. Guys in the dugouts were laughing as Kruk helplessly flailed, swinging at the next three pitches while staying away from the plate and far away from Randy's lethal fastball.

Two years later, in 1995, I was fortunate to start for the American League in my own stadium, The Ballpark in Arlington. That was a night that I will always treasure. And my backup for the game was Mike Stanley, who helped mentor me when I first came up and was so unselfish with his time. Both he and Geno Petralli treated me really well, and that was one of those lessons that came full circle with me when I signed with the Washington Nationals. I was ready when it was my time to pass along my knowledge to those who came next. So, sharing that moment with Mike was cool. I was really happy his career was going so well that he was named an All-Star. That man could hit.

In my family the 2000 All-Star Game is the one that is spoken about the most. And it wasn't because we won the game 6–3, though that was great since winning is always better than losing. During the Home Run Derby the night before the game, I may have accidentally left my son at Turner Field in Atlanta and gone back to my hotel. That sounds a lot worse than it really was. Well, at least that's my side of it.

Dereck's favorite player was Derek Jeter. Yes, even over me. I guess it was because they had the same first name. Trust me, it was awkward when he was running around the house wearing a New York Yankees jersey, but you try and make the kids happy, right?

Dereck Rodriguez
Son
"As far as I knew, Derek Jeter was the only other player with the name Derek. It was during that time when the Yankees

were the best team in baseball. I used to always say that he was my favorite player and at first I think I was kidding my father more than anything, but it kind of became true.

"One time that stands out, I remember we were on the team bus during All-Star week. It was me and my dad and all the other players. After my dad sat down, Derek Jeter saw me and motioned for me to come sit next to him. And I got to sit on the bus with him from the hotel to the stadium. Things like that made me like him even more because he was just a cool person."

I loved the atmosphere of Home Run Derby and all that goes along with it, but to be honest, it's a long night after what's already been a long day. I needed to wake up early for my workout, so I would usually leave after the first round—except for the years I participated in it. Besides, it's too long, and the best home-run hitters are usually exhausted by the end anyhow. That's a lot of swings.

Anyhow, like I was saying, my son and Derek Jeter were inseparable at those All-Star Games. So in 2000 they were on the field together before the derby started. I think they were playing a little catch, too. They seemed happy, and I didn't want to take my son away from having fun. I don't know, I guess, I just didn't really think it all out. I knew my wife was back at the hotel with the other two younger kids. I would love to say that I thought Jeter was going to bring him back, but I can't blame him. So, I snuck out, grabbed a taxi, and headed for the hotel. I walk in, and Maribel said, "Where's Dereck?"

I said, "I thought he was with you." And as I said it, I was thinking, *That doesn't make sense. She left before I did.* The next two words out of my mouth were, "Oh shit."

There's a lot of crap and chaos going on at the All-Star Game, but I still should have remembered my son. I took another taxi back to the stadium, and there he was. He was still in uniform, playing in the clubhouse with the other kids like nothing happened. Unlike at regular-season games, they let the kids come in there during All-Star events. They didn't let them go and shag balls in the outfield because a line drive or foul ball can hurt somebody, but they could be in the dugout and clubhouse.

A lot of people ask me about the best pitcher I ever faced or caught, and they will bring up guys from the All-Star Game. But that's tough. At the All-Star Game, you could obviously say those were some of the best pitchers. To me, though, the best meant a guy that I would feel comfortable catching for 100-plus innings a year.

The prime example for me was behind the plate at the 1999 All-Star Game in Boston. I caught Pedro Martinez for two innings, which was great, but that wasn't long enough to really get a feel for him. Pedro had some nasty stuff that day. He struck out five of the six batters he faced, including Barry Larkin, Jeff Bagwell, Sammy Sosa, Larry Walker, and Mark McGwire. The only batter he didn't strike out was Matt Williams, but I threw him out trying to steal second to end the second inning.

As far as facing them, there's no question Pedro was the best. He was unbelievable. Then there was Randy, Roger Clemens, and David Cone. I could not get a hit against Cone. Some days, you could give me all 27 at-bats against Cone, and I wouldn't reach first base. He had all those different angles and different pitches. If you ask me, the man was like a snowflake because he never threw the same pitch twice in his life. After facing so many pitchers and catching so many, I realized that if you're on the rubber at the major league level, it's because you're good. It's just that some hitters happen to hit certain pitchers better and vice versa.

But yes, All-Star Games were a lot of fun for us as a family. We always had a bunch of people there, and it was a much different feel than the regular season or playoffs. It was more laid-back with a lot more family fun. I know Dereck loved going to those games and seeing all the players, and he developed relationships with some of the other kids who were lucky enough to be there year after year.

In many ways Dereck grew up around baseball. He was always in the locker room. I remember when he was young, like a year old, and we were playing the Seattle Mariners, and Ken Griffey Jr. picked him up. I guess that made Dereck nervous because he peed all over his arm. That was pretty funny.

My sense of family goes back to my own parents and how they were with my brother and me. Even more than that, they instilled in us just how important family was, and that includes everyone from aunts and uncles to cousins and grandparents.

What makes this all the more remarkable from my parents is that they divorced a long time ago, when I was 12 years old. They got divorced, but they were still friendly, doing things right and wanting to make sure my brother and I didn't suffer. They were very polite and pleasant when talking to each other. If you see them today, they've both remarried, but they're best friends. My dad's home is behind my grandfather's home, and my mom remodeled my grandpa's house and goes there every weekend. She cooks, and they spend time together, so it's a very good relationship. We are so fortunate they were like that for our sake, and they set such a great example for everyone. They truly care about each other.

I think seeing my parents' divorce helped me deal with my own, which was certainly difficult as I already wrote about. Maribel is a great mom and a great person. I think one of the reasons that I played for so long in the big leagues is because I got married at 20 years old. Because if I didn't get married at 20, then I probably would have been single during my major league career. And I might have done things that I wasn't supposed to be doing like partying more or going out more often. I didn't do that. Dereck was born a year after we got married, and when that beautiful baby boy was in the house, it kept me at home because I didn't want to go anywhere. I just wanted to be with him. I just wanted to carry him around and be at the house taking care of him.

When Dereck was a year old, he was right next to me during the Rangers' team family day, and there were a couple pictures taken of us from the back. I was wearing my Rodriguez jersey, and he was wearing his Rodriguez jersey—two No. 7s walking together. Those are some cool pictures because we were both young. I was 20 and I had my one-year-old kid walking with me on the field. It was one of the coolest moments of my entire life.

I have another one where I'm sitting with my full catcher's gear on. It was during spring training in Port Charlotte, Florida, where the wives used to sit right next to the bullpen. Maribel said to me, "Dereck wants to come see you for a second." So, I was getting loose and stretching with all my gear on, waiting for the pitcher so I could catch him before the game, and Dereck was sitting right there in my lap.

Our relationship was similar to what I had with my dad. Dereck was in the clubhouse from the time he was a year old and he would cry on days I couldn't take him because he wanted to come with me. But it was great. When he was born, it kept me at home, playing with him and playing ball in the house.

When my daughter, Amanda, was born, that was something special because I never had a sister—only my brother. She's younger than Dereck by three years. If I was all over Dereck when he was born, it was twice as much with Amanda. Then our second daughter, Ivanna, was born a few years after Amanda. I love all three of my kids from the bottom of my heart, but all three are different. It's a unique, special love I have for the three of them.

I always loved being a father. That's why when I got divorced it was one of the hardest things in my life because I had always been with the kids. In the offseason I was with them 24/7. We traveled, we went on vacation, we were together every day for four and a half months. And knowing that I couldn't see them every day was the biggest pain that I felt. Or if I went to the house, I could see them just for a little bit and then had to leave again. Luckily, they could stay with me in Miami on the weekends.

Not being able to be with them was the hardest part. The same is true today, even though they are grown-ups. The conversations aren't the same as before because they're older now and they're adults, but when we are together, we have a great time. Amanda just moved to Dallas. She lives five minutes down the road, so I have her close now when I am in town.

Dereck

"My father during the season was not that different from the offseason because he knew how to switch it off when he was away from the field. He could go 0-for-4 and he'd be pissed after a game, but once he left that clubhouse, he could just brush it off like nothing happened. He was really good at doing that. During the season he was always focused and on

the field he knew what he had to do. During the offseason, though, he was a lot of fun. He was a goofball. I guess that was the only difference.

"When we lived in Miami, we would be at the pool almost every single day, hanging out, doing barbeques, and things like that. So that was always fun. We used to travel a lot. We went to Italy, and then when my dad had the boat, we took a month-long trip to all the Caribbean islands, Saint Barts, Saint Martin, all those places.

"When I was younger, he had to teach me a lot of things, but as I got more mature, the father-son thing started turning into more of a friendship. Even now, sometimes when we go out, he'll say, 'This is my little brother.' I wouldn't say he was strict. He just wanted me to do things the right way. I remember one game when I was 12 or 13 years old. I had the bottom of my pant legs pulled below my spikes, just baggy down there because that was the style. He let me have it after the game, telling me all about wearing the uniform the right way."

One of the proudest days of my life came when Dereck was selected by the Minnesota Twins in the sixth round of the 2011 Major League Baseball Draft. He was an outfielder at first, but now he's a pitcher, and he has some nasty stuff. I really hope he makes it and has a great career, but I just want him to be happy in life.

We were actually teammates in winter ball the spring before I retired. I was still thinking about maybe trying to play one more season and I also wanted to experience being on the same team as Dereck. We had an intrasquad game before the winter ball season started in Caguas, Puerto Rico. I was playing against Dereck's team, and he got a base hit.

And then he tried to steal against me on the very first pitch. I knew he would try to go because I saw that he was leaning toward second base. So, as a veteran, obviously I called for a fastball away. And there he went. I threw him out by 10 feet, and that's with me throwing the ball to the shortstop side of the base. The infielder had time to catch the ball to his right side, turn around, and wait for Dereck to arrive. It was funny because as he was running back to the dugout I was screaming at him from home plate. I told him, "Don't try that again!" That was cool. He was laughing, too. He said he had to try to steal a base off his father at least once.

Even though my three children were mostly raised in the United States, they only attended school here. My hometown played a big role in their lives. We spent the majority of our offseasons in Puerto Rico early in my career, too. We bought our first house in my hometown of Vega Baja, Puerto Rico, in 1991, the first year I got called up. Then the following year we bought another house in a gated community and then two or three years later we moved to San Juan.

TITO RODRIGUEZ
OLDER BROTHER

"Ivan is a big deal in Puerto Rico, just like Roberto Clemente and Orlando Cepeda. The reason he's reached that level isn't just because he was a great baseball player. It's because of the way he treats the people of the country and his fans. He always played winter ball here, he travels to Puerto Rico all the time, and I've never seen him say no to an autograph request or taking a photo. And he doesn't know how to say no when it comes to charity. Ivan will do five clinics and three charity events in a day. I've spent those days with him. It's exhausting, and I'm not even the one signing all the autographs and smiling for all the pictures. He's tireless when it comes to giving back for Puerto Rico. He has never, ever forgotten for a single day where he came from. That's why the people love him. Ivan is the kind of man we should all strive to be, and I can't say enough about him. I couldn't be more proud.

"And even with all his success and what a great father he is, Ivan can still act like a little boy. When it's just us, and there's nothing on TV, sometimes we will wrinkle up a piece of paper and use our sandals for the bat and play our game like we did when we were kids. We would play that until 3:00 AM some mornings and we still do."

During the season in Texas, I rented an apartment right next to the ballpark, and then a couple of years later, we bought a house in nearby Colleyville, where the kids went to school. All three kids were born in Texas, and we lived there for a while. We were also there in the offseason because of school for the kids. We didn't buy a place in Miami until later, maybe in 1997 or 1998. That's when I bought an apartment in the Brickell neighborhood. Then we saw a house by the water in 2000 that we loved and we lived there for five years. It was still under construction at that time, but we spent pretty much the whole season in Miami.

I played winter ball in Puerto Rico every December. I was there every last month of the year. When school ended a week before Christmas, the kids would come down and spend a few weeks there. Sometimes during the season, or when we would go and travel, we would take a schoolteacher with us for the kids. We took the teacher with us when we went to Italy. The kids would study in the morning, and then after that, they would have the whole day free.

I met Patricia Gomez after I separated. She was a lot like me. She had three kids of her own from another marriage. Patricia is from Colombia, but she was living in Miami. We actually met in her brother Ivan's restaurant. She traveled with me on the road whenever she could. I always like having company, and we obviously spent a lot of time together during the offseason.

We were married on February 7, 2007, in Miami and we renewed our vows in Puerto Rico four years later. When we first met, Patricia knew absolutely nothing about baseball. Like nothing. She didn't know the difference between me going 4-for-4 or 0-for-4. I would say, "Patricia, I had two hits and two RBIs today and threw out a base runner," and she would say, "I'm sorry, honey."

"No, no," I would tell her, "that's a good game." And then she'd be happy. It was cute.

PATRICIA GOMEZ
WIFE

"When I'd see a catcher on TV, I would always think it was Ivan. I would tell the people I was watching the game with, 'That's Ivan.' And they would say, 'No, that's the other catcher.' They all looked the same to me in the mask and gear.

"It's really been a struggle to regulate his sleep. He tells me he's been like that his whole life. It's not easy, but I am convinced it can be done. Just not yet. He just always has so much energy. We would eat late after the game, and I would be tired, but he would stay up watching TV until the wee hours.

"Still, I admire him so much for being disciplined and dedicated to his training. It didn't matter when he went to bed, he'd get up to exercise early and would go to the ballpark early. And he was usually one of the last players to leave. I'd be waiting there when everyone else was gone, asking, 'Where is Ivan?' He was working out or putting together the scouting report for the next series. No one ever gave Ivan anything in his career. He is a work machine. He worked so hard because of his passion and love for the game."

Patricia also thought the games were too long, which sometimes they are, but that never bothered me. She came to more and more of my games as her kids grew older. She now has four grandchildren, too, and they're wonderful to spend time with. We are incredibly happy together and we stay busy.

We try and visit Colombia as often as we can. I love the weather and love seeing her family. Who doesn't love being a grandfather? I thank God every day that I found Patricia and have been able to share these years with her and our family. To her, I'm not a famous, successful baseball player. I'm a man who laughs and cries and who has gone through a lot of tough times. And she's been there for me and made my life so much better.

My life and family has been so much about baseball. We have all been so fortunate this game came into my life. When parents and kids ask me for advice, the first thing I tell them is to have them play sports they enjoy. Sports is the best way to live a dedicated life toward fitness and team play, and stay involved with it throughout your life.

15

A Catcher's Legacy

I THINK THAT MAYBE SOME PEOPLE, WHEN THEY READ A BOOK about someone they know—be it an athlete, a movie star, or a politician—they expect to read about parties at these extravagant places with these famous people. And they expect to read about all the money. And maybe along the way, if you're lucky, the author will throw a few people under the bus. There's your book.

First off, I'm not holding out on the parties. I wasn't there. Go ahead, Google "Pudge Rodriguez" and "partying," and I promise it's going to be a quick search. Now, if you Google just "Pudge" and "partying" without my last name, that could be a little more entertaining, but you still won't see me anywhere.

I am a pretty boring guy. I played the game I loved so much and I played it with all my intensity, which I could control at least most of the time. They say to become an expert in any field in life you have to commit 10,000 hours to it. My guess is that I had played 10,000 hours of baseball before I was a teenager. And I had probably watched 10,000 hours of it by then, too. By the time the Texas Rangers called me up at 19 after a few seasons in the minor leagues, I had probably played more than 25,000 hours of baseball. And that doesn't include workouts designed to help me play baseball.

From a very young age, I knew there was one thing I wanted to do in life, and that was baseball. I fell asleep at night thinking about baseball. I woke up, and my first thought was baseball. When I brushed my teeth, I was thinking about baseball. When I was in school, I was thinking about baseball. I would say from my birth until I retired, 95 percent of what I watched on television was baseball. The other 5 percent was whatever else came on after the baseball game I was watching. Baseball wasn't my hobby. Baseball wasn't my occupation. Baseball wasn't a game and baseball wasn't a business. Baseball was my obsession. Baseball was my life. And I want it to be a part of my life until the day I leave this great world for the next. My life has been pretty simple: God, family, and baseball.

So, I haven't really held anything back in this book. It's just that, well, I'm pretty much a single-minded guy. Once in a while, maybe Juan Gonzalez and I would go have a beer or two earlier in my career, but if my family was in town, I wanted to go see them. Sometimes we would go out with our wives, but that's about it.

It's difficult to wake up every morning and work out on limited sleep if you drank too much the night before. That workout was my everything. I tell kids all the time to make it part of their routine. That workout every morning was like me brushing my teeth or taking a shower. It's not like people decide to take a month off from doing those things, so why would you take a month off from the workout? I needed to work out. I needed every advantage possible to succeed. And I also wanted to do it as long as possible. You hear about guys like Tom Brady and Dirk Nowitzki, who is a wonderful man I know from being in Dallas. You see them playing at a high level at 38, 39, and hopefully 40 years old and beyond for both of them. And you hear about the special diets, the hydration, and not drinking alcohol. That's not a coincidence.

I set my standard pretty high. It's one thing to say, "Yeah, I want to be an All-Star, I want to win a Gold Glove, I want to play in 150 games, I want to win a World Series." These are all high and lofty goals that probably 1 percent of big league players attain. My goal was a little different, though. I say "goal," but that's probably the wrong word. It wasn't a goal as much as a way of life, a commitment to strive toward the excellence and greatness of two men: Johnny Bench and Roberto Clemente.

If I were starting my own all-time dream team, I would start with those two—as both players and men. Johnny was my idol growing up. There is no greater honor I will ever have in this world than joining him as the only first-ballot Hall of Fame catchers. Know what means almost just as much, though? What he said a few days before the vote. He said, "If Pudge doesn't go into the Hall of Fame this year, I don't know what these people are doing."

That truly moved me. In all my stress and anxiety, those words calmed me, and I thought of them often. Johnny and I have been to a few events, card shows, and other things like that. And every time we see each other backstage or signing autographs, we talk a little while. I always tell him how happy I am to see him. Hopefully, now that we will be seeing each other every year in Cooperstown, we will become even closer. Maybe we can play some golf together. That would mean so much to me.

As a catcher, as a baseball player, that was my standard. I wanted to play like the great Johnny Bench. I wanted to throw out base runners like the great Johnny Bench. I wanted to win the World Series like the great Johnny Bench. Johnny played in a different era than I did. I came in eight seasons after he retired in 1983. I hope I maintained that position proudly, at that level. To me, the catching position can fly a little under the radar. People don't know how much and how hard we work. As a catcher you have to study the game, come to the ballpark early, make sure you look at every single report, watch video, and talk with the pitching coach. And then after talking to the pitching coach, you go and talk to the pitcher about the gameplan that you have.

It's not just catching and throwing. It's not blocking or a play at the plate or some collision. No, the biggest part of the game as a catcher is making sure those fingers you put down are the right ones. When you're working with another mind, that being the pitcher, you can put the minds together and have a beautiful gameplan. If the battery is connected like that, the games become magical.

To have an official club, you need at least two, and now we have our selective club of first-ballot catchers. It's just me and Johnny. What can I say? I think back to my childhood in Puerto Rico, growing up, looking at this little television, and telling everyone, "I am going to be like Johnny Bench someday." And then one day, I'm being recognized on the same level as him, right next to him. That is the stuff of dreams. If you turned that into a movie, people would laugh. They would say it couldn't happen. Well, look at me. Dream big and work hard and don't ever, ever, ever let anyone tell you what can't be accomplished.

In Puerto Rico, when I was growing up and even more so now, Clemente was more than an idol or your typical baseball hero. He was more of a god, not only for the way he played, the way he carried himself, and the way he paved the way for all Latino players, but also for the way he gave of himself, his time, and his money for those less fortunate.

You hear the stories growing up. They tell stories of the great Clemente like they do nursery rhymes and fairy tales. It's not only the 3,000 hits, the batting titles, the Gold Gloves, the championships with the Pittsburgh Pirates, but also how he returned to our country every offseason, how he spent countless hours with the children, how he brought food to those who needed to be fed, and how he gave his own money to help those who were impoverished. As we all know, that's how he died, which makes it even more tragic. The plane he was on probably went down because it was carrying too much food and too much help for those in Nicaragua, following the devastating earthquake that struck that country. He had heard that the first three planes he filled with food and medical supplies had been taken by corrupt government officials, and little or none of it reached the intended victims who were in need. So, he jumped aboard a plane himself to make sure the supplies arrived, and the plane went down off the coast of Puerto Rico. He was 38 years old, married with three young children of his own. That was New Year's Eve of 1972, just 13 months after I was born.

Every day when I took the field, I tried to honor Clemente's memory. And when I made the big leagues and they would ask for volunteers for charity work, outreach programs, or baseball clinics for kids, I would always raise my hand. They told me that I didn't have to do all of them, that some of the guys didn't do any of them, but being from Puerto Rico, I needed to honor Roberto Clemente and the man he was. So, from when I was a rookie to when I was the old man on the team, I kept raising my hand. Eric Nadel, Rangers radio announcer, told *The Dallas Morning News:* "The Pudge moment I will never forget came on a Rangers off day, Wednesday, September 10, 1997, at a Methodist church in Arlington. It was at the funeral for Mark Holtz, the Rangers TV broadcaster who had died after a bout with leukemia. As I looked around the church, I spotted a solitary figure in the section reserved for active Rangers players. There sat Rodriguez all by himself. I called Jeff Kuster, who's married to Holtz's daughter,

Cindy, on Thursday to ask if any other active Rangers player attended the funeral. Kuster didn't know. He had other things on his mind that day. But he volunteered to find and check the sign-in book. When he called back, Kuster reported that only one player signed the book. 'It was Ivan Rodriguez,' he said. 'We never knew.'"

I never kept awards when I was playing. My father has most of that stuff now. I don't have any baseballs or catcher's mitts either. I know there's a Gold Glove or two in Florida at my house there. I always kept the catcher's mitt I used for any Gold Glove season, so I guess those might be there as well. Again, my father and brother have a bunch of that. The American League MVP award is in Colombia with my wife's family, so I can check in on it a few times a year, just to make sure it knows I'm still around. I'm guessing someone has the Silver Slugger awards, I'm just not sure exactly who.

Don't get me wrong, I am incredibly proud of my career. It's just that, well, how can I say this? I know what I did and I also know this: I didn't do it for the awards and the numbers. Those were by-products. I put in the work I did because I wanted to make sure the sacrifices my parents made were honored, so that I could play the game I loved, so that I could push myself to be like Johnny Bench and Roberto Clemente.

That's why I don't need the awards to remind me. Other people enjoy having them and showing them off, and I like to make other people happy. And it's more than the awards. It's the legacy we leave behind, the example we set for the next generation and the one after that. "Everybody wanted to be like Pudge," said Geovany Soto, All-Star catcher from Puerto Rico. "He was a national hero, man. He was unbelievable, that ideal childhood icon you looked up to."

I will look back on some highlights now and again, mostly when I fly. I'll pull out my Apple laptop and watch myself from 1991, my rookie season, right through that last year. I think we all like to look back and remember the good times. Know what my favorite part is? When I am high-fiving and hugging my teammates. There is a connection you make with those guys that is impossible to explain. It's a lifelong bond. If I see a guy from 20 years ago, we aren't shaking hands. We're giving each other a big hug. When you work together for this common goal for seven months, there's an emotional bond that evolves and really never leaves. It's all about the success of the team. That is every player's goal, and it's a team effort from Day One in spring training. It's that seven or eight-month grind, the good and bad, the ups and downs.

I had a full physical a few weeks after the Hall of Fame vote, and the doctor looked at my back and said, "I've never seen a 45-year-old spine and lower back the way you have it. You're in great shape." And that's not just after 25 years of pro ball either. I've been catching since I was seven years old. I was squatting from age seven to age 40. And my knees never really bothered me. There's some luck involved there, but it's also because of the stretching and work I did when I wasn't catching. You so often hear people talk about how they just didn't catch the breaks. Well, you have to make your own breaks with hard work and sacrifice.

This is a point in my life where I'm kind of thinking about what's next. I am involved in a lot of business. I fly probably half the year for business, clinics, and appearances. I do a lot of charity work with Buzz Off Kids For Cancer, San Jorge Children's Hospital, Posada de Moises, and for years I had my own, the Pudge Rodriguez Foundation.

I've been doing the Rangers' pregame show for home games the last three years and have been hoping to maybe land a national gig, so we'll see how that goes. I also spend time working with the other catchers in the Rangers' organization. I especially enjoy working with the younger ones in the lower ranks of the minor leagues. The Hall of Fame was a big thing. I think I was kind of waiting to see how that went and when it happened, I thought, *Let's focus on this. Let's do a book, tell my story, and then maybe take a moment after Cooperstown to see what the options are.*

I've never talked about this previously, but managing is something that really interests me. Every time I go to the Miami Marlins games and see my old Cigar Man, Jack McKeon, he tells me, "I want to see you manage, Pudge. You would be a good one." That's high praise coming from him, and my other former skippers agree.

JIM LEYLAND
TIGERS MANAGER
"I think he could be a heck of a manager. He needs to be patient because a big part of managing a baseball team is patience. I would love to see him get some experience, maybe do a few seasons in the minor leagues. Now, if he doesn't want to do that, there have been some guys who have bypassed that, and it's worked out. The Tigers have a great young manager who didn't manage beforehand in Brad Ausmus. Pudge has the skillset. He's one of the smartest ballplayers I've ever managed, and we'd talk all the time about strategy, and he brought up stuff that never entered my mind and he was usually right. Pudge saw the game differently than a lot of guys. His mind was so quick and instinctive. He just knew the decision to make, and it

took him a second to make it. I could see him being a really successful manager."

I do think about it. I'm not going to lie, I think about it often. When the time comes, it's something I hope is in my future. I could do it, I promise you that. Catchers are always good managers.

DERECK RODRIGUEZ
SON
"I think he'd be a fantastic manager. He hasn't talked about it, but I know him better than anybody. He wants to get back in a uniform and travel. But he just doesn't want to go through the whole process. If he's going to be a manager, he wants to be a big league manager. He doesn't want to go to the minor leagues. He wants to be on top right away. He'd be such a great manager.

"Even when he was playing, he was always planning ahead, like not trying to pick guys off when the No. 8 or 9 batter is up. You don't want to start off the next inning with the leadoff guy and you want the 3-4-5 hitters up when there's nobody on base. It's like playing chess, honestly. He just did it by instinct. When he used to do that stuff, he probably didn't even think about it. It was just natural. He would blow my mind sometimes with how he saw the game being played out."

The night before the Hall of Fame vote was announced in January 2017, that was one of the most anxious nights of my life. Those were a hard couple of days. I can't even explain how stressed out I was. I don't sleep much as is, but it was nonexistent that week. I was up for like 72 straight hours. The lone upside was having time to reflect, having time to think about baseball being the best game on the planet and all these extraordinary catchers who came before me. You cannot beat that.

I have so much respect for those great catchers who had to wait for induction. Unbelievable names like Carlton Fisk, Gary Carter, Mickey Cochrane, and Yogi Berra. Before he passed away, Yogi saw me a long time ago when I was playing in Yankee Stadium. During batting practice he looked at me in the eyes and told me, "You're going to be a Hall of Famer." That was huge. That gave me chills. I couldn't tell you anything about the game, but I walked out of the locker room that night smiling because of what Yogi Berra told me.

Berra's teammate Mickey Mantle, who lived in Dallas most of his life, wore No. 7 for the New York Yankees. I love the No. 7, but I didn't ask for it. In the minor leagues, I used No. 10 and then I was No. 55 when I was put on the 40-man roster. But the number that I really, really loved was No. 10.

Anyway, when they called me up in June 1991, I was 19 and I wasn't going to be some cocky kid demanding a certain number or anything. I barely spoke English, so I took what they gave me, which was No. 7. The next year my plan was to ask for a new number, No. 10, but veteran infielder Dickie Thon had joined the team, and he was wearing it. So I just said, "Okay, I'll stick with No. 7." Dickie was gone by the next year, but I said, "No, I'm going to stay with No. 7." It's a lucky number for some people. I feel like I didn't want to have a two-digit number on my back anyway. I'm not too tall, so two numbers on the back is not going to look right on me.

I tried to sleep the night before the Hall of Fame vote and I at least got into the bed for an hour or two. I woke up early and did my workout like I always do, staying with my routine. I spent most of the day after that at home, not watching any TV, trying to stay away from what was happening. A lot of people were texting me, and I was texting them back, but I had to tell them, "Look, you have to wait until the afternoon."

Then we left the house at about 4:00 or 4:15 to go to my friend's house about five minutes away. And that's where I was, waiting for the call. Dereck was there; my wife was there; my friend and his wife, Mike and Melissa Allen, were there; and my agent, Catalina Villegas, was there. And ESPN was there with me, too. I was doing an interview with them when I got the phone call.

Hall president Jeff Idelson and Baseball Writers' Association of America secretary-treasurer Jack O'Connell congratulated me over the phone for becoming a member of the 2017 Hall of Fame. I received information about the logistics of getting to the ballpark and then flying to New York that night. Commissioner Rob Manfred even called to congratulate me.

We got on the plane at about 9:30 PM. It was me, my wife, my son, and Catalina and it was past midnight when we landed. Then we had breakfast in the morning with everyone followed by a press conference. From there we went to the MLB Network studios and then we had a very small, private dinner after that.

I went to Cooperstown, New York, three weeks later. I've been there four times now. We walked through the museum again, and I was shown where my plaque is going to be. When I retired, yes, I was thinking about having my plaque in Cooperstown. During my career, though, I didn't think about being in the Hall of Fame. Instead I was thinking about having great years and having a great career. And then the career took me to another level, and that level was to be in the Hall of Fame. But to be honest, I didn't think I was going to get in on the first ballot. I really didn't. Not that I didn't deserve it, I just didn't think it was going to happen. It was a gift because there aren't too many first-ballot Hall of Famers, especially for catchers.

Being elected on the first try meant even more knowing that Tim Raines waited 10 years and Jeff Bagwell waited seven years. That's a long time. So, getting into the Hall of Fame on the first ballot was a pretty cool thing, and I'm very grateful. My phone went crazy after the vote. At one point I had almost a thousand text messages from friends and former players and I answered every single one of them. I'm still getting some texts and e-mails. I appreciate all of them.

I even heard from Johnny Bench. I got messages from Jim Leyland and a bunch of other managers that I played for, former players, active players, superstars of today. Almost the entire Rangers team and coaching staff called or texted me. Every single text meant so much, and everyone was very happy that I got in.

It's been a great experience, and I think it's a great achievement to be in the Hall of Fame. It changes pretty much everything, having "Hall of Famer" next to my name forever. Everywhere I go now, it's not going to be "Pudge, the great baseball player." Now it's going to be "Pudge, the Hall of Famer." It will also be nice to join Nolan Ryan and Johnny Oates as the only people to have our jersey numbers retired by the Rangers. And, of course, Jackie Robinson, whose No. 42 is retired across baseball. Every time I sit there at the ballpark, I can look up and see my last name and number on display. They are going to retire it shortly after I am inducted in Cooperstown. It's going to be quite the year for me.

I went to Puerto Rico after the Hall of Fame results were announced, and that's where I saw my dad for the first time since the vote. It was great. We got to the airport, and all the family was there. They let them come past the gate, so everyone was waiting for me when I got off the plane. Everything they did in Puerto Rico was very organized, which helped me get to the places I needed to be and do the things I needed to do. I probably took a photo with every resident of Puerto Rico that week I was down there and I was happy to do so.

My family is still very happy and very emotional. Obviously, I am, too. It's a great thing, especially since I had two parents who were with me—day in and day out—since Day One. When my brother and I were growing up, my parents would practice with us every Tuesday and Thursday and then be with me and my brother the whole day Saturday. One would go to see my brother play, and the other would come to see me. And then when the second game started, they would switch. Even when I was playing in the big leagues, my dad would come three or four times a year and stay with me for a couple weeks. Sometimes he would even travel with the team, and my mom did, too. They love baseball. And I love them so much. They paved the way for my success.

I was reading some of the stories after I was voted into the Hall of Fame. Yes, as much as athletes and coaches say they don't read stuff in the media, most of them usually do, though I wasn't obsessed like some were during my playing days. I felt like I had a good relationship with the press. I talked to them whenever they asked me questions. And I really tried to be honest, too. They have a job to do just like me, and I respected that.

Anyway, one of the constant topics of the stories I was reading was my ever-present smile when I was playing baseball. You don't always see that, I guess, but here's the thing: I wasn't conscious of my smiling. I guess I was just happy. I was in my happy place, playing this game I so respected and adored.

John Blake
Rangers Executive Vice President
of Communications

"His popularity stems from his whole body of work, on and off the field. The autographs, the clinics with the kids, his youthful exuberance. There were some years he was the best player on the team, but he was always part of a bigger core that included guys like Juan Gonzalez, Rafael Palmeiro, Will Clark, and Rusty Greer. Our best teams were built around strong cores. Looking back at those rosters now, you say, 'Wow, they had Ivan Rodriguez.' He's going to be remembered as the only Hall of Famer from those division-winning 1990s teams. But in those days, it was more of a team, and he was an MVP and an All-Star, and his presence kind of became a given. I remember the first year we didn't have him, in 2003. That's when we realized how much we took him for granted. We didn't have to worry about the running game when he played for all those years. He was so dominant behind the plate, you almost forgot how much better he was than every other catcher.

"But again, it's his smile that stands out. When we run highlights of him, you can see it. If you're a real Rangers fan from that era, you remember how much fun Pudge had playing the game. The pictures of him, the fist pumping, the time he went over to the seats and ate a fan's nachos, just things like that. And he always had that smile, even when he was 19. He always looked like he had fun playing the game. He was popular back then and he would get a big ovation, but now it's carried over to where if you marched all the former Rangers players out there, it's going to be Nolan Ryan and Pudge with the loudest ovations."

I want to make sure this is stated correctly, so for starters, I have the utmost admiration for every team I spent time with in my career. The Florida (now Miami) Marlins allowed me to let the baseball world know that I wasn't on the downside of my career, and we were able to shock everyone by winning the World Series. Those few weeks of the 2003 postseason were the most rewarding of my career. The Detroit Tigers gave me a chance to help turn around that proud franchise, the opportunity to play for Jim Leyland—one of the best to ever manage—and to return to the Fall Classic. The honor was all mine, Detroit.

The New York Yankees let me play for that organization, for those fans, and there is no higher honor the game has than to play in the home pinstripes at Yankee Stadium. The Houston Astros took a chance on an aging catcher, and I gave them my best effort. I worked as hard that season as I did as a rookie. They love their baseball in Houston. The Washington Nationals let me finish my career with that great group of guys, work with the younger players, and see the city fall in love with baseball all over again after not having a team for so long. That was a lasting thrill, which will stay with me forever.

My heart, though, belongs with the Texas Rangers. They signed me. I spent 14-plus years of my professional life with them, I grew up there, and I am proud to wear their cap forever in the Hall of Fame. The Rangers always treated me first class, and I did everything within my power to return the gesture and carry myself first class. I hope the team and the fans believe I accomplished just that.

There are two more stories I'd like to share. I think they kind of explain why I was able to accomplish what I did. I'm not exactly sure of the year, but at spring training, it had rained the night before, and a few of us walked onto the field early, when the tarps were still covering the pitcher's mound and home plate area. We were just having some fun when someone tried to throw a ball from behind the plate, off the mound, to second base. The ball skidded off the slick tarp into foul territory.

Of course, I was always up for a challenge. I took a ball, crouched behind the plate, came up throwing, and hit the mound precisely. The ball bounced right off the mound and landed in my teammate's glove at the second-base bag. I smiled and walked off the field. I think they call that dropping the mic nowadays.

Later in my career, I was with the Yankees and I was really sick. This was in early August 2008, just a few days after I was traded to them. I couldn't even get out of bed. I felt like death. I guess it was the flu or food poisoning, I still don't know. My father and wife were in town. It was so bad that my father literally had to help me into the shower. I couldn't even walk on my own.

I wanted to play, though, since we were in a playoff race. I didn't like taking anything for pain, but Patricia convinced me to take a few Advil. I somehow made it to the park, where the trainers hydrated me the best they could. I played, I hit a home run, and we won the game. Here's my point: to succeed in anything in this world, you need some talent, you need some luck, and you need some courage. And working your ass off in between is only going to increase your chances.

Finally, if you ever see me around, don't feel intimidated to ask me for an autograph or a picture. You're not putting me out. It's my honor. Tell me your favorite Pudge story. Chances are, it's going to put a smile on my face. And you know how much I like to smile.

Appendix

Appendix I: Regular-Season Batting

Year	Age	Tm	Lg	G	AB	R	H	2B	3B	HR	RBI	SB	BB	SO	BA	OBP	SLG	OPS
1991	19	TEX	AL	88	280	24	74	16	0	3	27	0	5	42	.264	.276	.354	.630
1992	20	TEX	AL	123	420	39	109	16	1	8	37	0	24	73	.260	.300	.360	.659
1993	21	TEX	AL	137	473	56	129	28	4	10	66	8	29	70	.273	.315	.412	.727
1994	22	TEX	AL	99	363	56	108	19	1	16	57	6	31	42	.298	.360	.488	.848
1995	23	TEX	AL	130	492	56	149	32	2	12	67	0	16	48	.303	.327	.449	.776
1996	24	TEX	AL	153	639	116	192	47	3	19	86	5	38	55	.300	.342	.473	.814
1997	25	TEX	AL	150	597	98	187	34	4	20	77	7	38	89	.313	.360	.484	.844
1998	26	TEX	AL	145	579	88	186	40	4	21	91	9	32	88	.321	.358	.513	.871
1999	27	TEX	AL	144	600	116	199	29	1	35	113	25	24	64	.332	.356	.558	.914
2000	28	TEX	AL	91	363	66	126	27	4	27	83	5	19	48	.347	.375	.667	1.042
2001	29	TEX	AL	111	442	70	136	24	2	25	65	10	23	73	.308	.347	.541	.888
2002	30	TEX	AL	108	408	67	128	32	2	19	60	5	25	71	.314	.353	.542	.895
2003	31	FLA	NL	144	511	90	152	36	3	16	85	10	55	92	.297	.369	.474	.843
2004	32	DET	AL	135	527	72	176	32	2	19	86	7	41	91	.334	.383	.510	.893
2005	33	DET	AL	129	504	71	139	33	5	14	50	7	11	93	.276	.290	.444	.735
2006	34	DET	AL	136	547	74	164	28	4	13	69	8	26	86	.300	.332	.437	.769
2007	35	DET	AL	129	502	50	141	31	3	11	63	2	9	96	.281	.294	.420	.714

Continued on next page

Year	Age	Tm	Lg	G	AB	R	H	2B	3B	HR	RBI	SB	BB	SO	BA	OBP	SLG	OPS
2008	36	TOT	AL	115	398	44	110	20	3	7	35	10	23	67	.276	.319	.394	.714
2008	36	DET	AL	82	302	33	89	16	3	5	32	6	19	52	.295	.338	.417	.756
2008	36	NYY	AL	33	96	11	21	4	0	2	3	4	4	15	.219	.257	.323	.580
2009	37	TOT	MLB	121	425	55	106	23	2	10	47	1	18	92	.249	.280	.384	.663
2009	37	HOU	NL	93	327	41	82	15	2	8	34	0	13	74	.251	.280	.382	.662
2009	37	TEX	AL	28	98	14	24	8	0	2	13	1	5	18	.245	.279	.388	.667
2010	38	WSN	NL	111	398	32	106	18	1	4	49	2	16	66	.266	.294	.347	.640
2011	39	WSN	NL	44	124	14	27	7	0	2	19	0	10	28	.218	.281	.323	.604
21 Yrs				2543	9592	1354	2844	572	51	311	1332	127	513	1474	**.296**	**.334**	**.464**	**.798**
162 Game Avg.				162	611	86	181	36	3	20	85	8	33	94	**.296**	**.334**	**.464**	**.798**
TEX (13 yrs)				1507	5754	866	1747	352	28	217	842	81	309	781	.304	.341	.488	.828
DET (5 yrs)				611	2382	300	709	140	17	62	300	30	106	418	.298	.328	.449	.777
WSN (2 yrs)				155	522	46	133	25	1	6	68	2	26	94	.255	.291	.341	.632
NYY (1 yr)				33	96	11	21	4	0	2	3	4	4	15	.219	.257	.323	.580
HOU (1 yr)				93	327	41	82	15	2	8	34	0	13	74	.251	.280	.382	.662
FLA (1 yr)				144	511	90	152	36	3	16	85	10	55	92	.297	.369	.474	.843
AL (18 yrs)				2151	8232	1177	2477	496	45	281	1145	115	419	1214	.301	.336	.474	.810
NL (4 yrs)				392	1360	177	367	76	6	30	187	12	94	260	.270	.319	.401	.720

Appendix II: Postseason Batting

Year	Tm	Series	Opp	Rslt	G	AB	R	H	2B	3B	HR	RBI	BB	SO	BA	OBP	SLG	OPS
1996	TEX	ALDS	NYY	L	4	16	1	6	1	0	0	2	2	3	.375	.444	.438	.882
1998	TEX	ALDS	NYY	L	3	10	0	1	0	0	0	1	0	5	.100	.100	.100	.200
1999	TEX	ALDS	NYY	L	3	12	0	3	1	0	0	0	0	2	.250	.250	.333	.583
2003	FLA	NLDS	SFG	W	4	17	3	6	1	0	1	6	3	1	.353	.450	.588	1.038
2003 MVP	FLA	NLCS	CHC	W	7	28	5	9	2	0	2	10	5	7	.321	.424	.607	1.031
2003	FLA	WS	NYY	W	6	22	2	6	2	0	0	1	1	4	.273	.292	.364	.655
2006	DET	ALDS	NYY	W	4	13	3	3	1	0	0	3	2	3	.231	.313	.308	.620
2006	DET	ALCS	OAK	W	4	16	2	2	0	0	1	1	1	4	.125	.176	.313	.489
2006	DET	WS	STL	L	5	19	1	3	1	0	0	1	0	3	.158	.158	.211	.368
5 Yrs (9 Series)					40	153	17	39	9	0	4	25	14	32	.255	.314	.392	.706
4 ALDS					14	51	4	13	3	0	0	6	4	13	.255	.304	.314	.617
1 NLDS					4	17	3	6	1	0	1	6	3	1	.353	.450	.588	1.038
1 NLCS					7	28	5	9	2	0	2	10	5	7	.321	.424	.607	1.031
1 ALCS					4	16	2	2	0	0	1	1	1	4	.125	.176	.313	.489
2 WS					11	41	3	9	3	0	0	2	1	7	.220	.233	.293	.525

Appendix III: Fielding

Year	Tm	Lg	Age	Pos	G	E	Fld%	Stolen Bases	Caught Stealing	Caught Stealing%	LeagueCS%
1991	TEX	AL	19	C	88	10	.983	36	34	49%	34%
1992	TEX	AL	20	C	116	15	.983	53	57	52%	34%
1992	TEX	AL	20	DH	2						
1993	TEX	AL	21	C	134	8	.991	64	51	44%	36%
1993	TEX	AL	21	DH	1						
1994	TEX	AL	22	C	99	5	.992	37	23	38%	31%
1995	TEX	AL	23	C	127	8	.990	40	37	48%	31%
1995	TEX	AL	23	DH	1						
1996	TEX	AL	24	C	146	10	.989	46	48	51%	30%
1996	TEX	AL	24	DH	6						
1997	TEX	AL	25	C	143	7	.992	37	49	57%	33%
1997	TEX	AL	25	DH	5						
1998	TEX	AL	26	C	139	6	.994	38	49	56%	31%
1998	TEX	AL	26	DH	6						
1999	TEX	AL	27	C	141	7	.993	34	41	55%	33%
1999	TEX	AL	27	DH	1						
2000	TEX	AL	28	C	87	2	.996	20	19	49%	30%

Continued on next page

Year	Tm	Lg	Age	Pos	G	E	Fld%	Stolen Bases	Caught Stealing	Caught Stealing%	LeagueCS%
2000	TEX	AL	28	DH	1						
2001	TEX	AL	29	C	106	7	.990	23	35	60%	29%
2001	TEX	AL	29	DH	5						
2002	TEX	AL	30	C	100	7	.990	26	15	37%	32%
2002	TEX	AL	30	DH	6						
2003	FLA	NL	31	C	138	8	.992	40	20	33%	31%
2003	FLA	NL	31	DH	1						
2004	DET	AL	32	C	124	11	.987	40	19	32%	32%
2004	DET	AL	32	DH	8						
2005	DET	AL	33	C	123	4	.995	33	35	51%	30%
2005	DET	AL	33	DH	3						
2006	DET	AL	34	C	123	2	.998	25	26	51%	30%
2006	DET	AL	34	1B	7	1	.984				
2006	DET	AL	34	DH	5						
2006	DET	AL	34	2B	1	0	1.000				
2007	DET	AL	35	C	127	6	.993	47	21	31%	27%
2007	DET	AL	35	DH	1						
2008	TOT	AL	36	C	112	5	.993	52	25	32%	27%

Continued on next page

Year	Tm	Lg	Age	Pos	G	E	Fld%	Stolen Bases	Caught Stealing	Caught Stealing%	LeagueCS%
2008	DET	AL	36	C	81	4	.992	32	18	36%	27%
2008	NYY	AL	36	C	31	1	.995	20	7	26%	27%
2008	NYY	AL	36	DH	2						
2009	TOT	MLB	37	C	115	7	.992	41	22	35%	28%
2009	HOU	NL	37	C	90	4	.994	34	16	32%	29%
2009	TEX	AL	37	C	25	3	.984	7	6	46%	26%
2009	TEX	AL	37	DH	3						
2010	WSN	NL	38	C	102	4	.995	42	22	34%	29%
2011	WSN	NL	39	C	37	3	.989	12	13	52%	28%
2011	WSN	NL	39	1B	1	0	1.000				
21 Seasons				C	2427	142	.991	786	661	46%	31%
17 Seasons				DH	57						
2 Seas ons				1B	8	1	.984				
1 Season				2B	1	0	1.000				
21 Seasons				TOT	2436	143	.991	786	661	46%	31%

Acknowledgments

Ivan Rodriguez

I must start with my home country, Puerto Rico, and the beautiful baseball fans that fill the island. The passion of that environment played a significant role in my success, not to mention allowed me to enjoy such a magical childhood.

My family is my everything. There is my best friend and rock, my wife, Patricia; my parents, Jose and Eva; my brother, Tito; my magnificent children, Dereck, Amanda, and Ivanna.

I was extremely fortunate to play for great men: owners like George W. Bush and Tom Schieffer in Texas, Jeffrey Loria in Florida, the late, great Mike Ilitch in Detroit, and Tom Lerner in Washington; general managers like Tom Grieve and Doug Melvin with the Rangers and Dave Dombrowski with the Tigers; and managers like Bobby Valentine, Kevin Kennedy, the late, great Johnny Oates, Jerry Narron, Jack McKeon, Alan Trammell, and Jim Leyland. Also, my longtime hitting coach, Rudy Jaramillo, I owe him so much for all he did for my swing.

I was even more fortunate to play with great men, my teammates. Rather than forget one or two and feel guilty for eternity, I'm just going to say there has been no greater honor in my life than playing with those I did, especially those who I did for several seasons. It's hard to describe to someone who hasn't experienced it, spending 10 or more hours a day for eight months with the same guys. It's a lot of fun, too.

I also want to thank Texas Rangers vice president of communications John Blake for everything he has done for me over the years and to this day. Also with the Rangers, Ray Davis, Bob Simpson, and Jon Daniels. My deepest appreciation to Baseball Hall of Fame president Jeff Idelson and MLB commissioner Rob Manfred.

This book also wouldn't have been possible without Tom Bast at Triumph Books and Catalina Villegas, who on top of everything else she does, really pushed me to do this. And I'm glad I did.

JEFF SULLIVAN

For the most part, Pudge's family and friends shielded him from the vote in terms of the information that was out there—mostly via the Baseball Hall of Fame tracker run by Ryan Thibodaux. When I met with Ivan the night before the vote for an interview for this book, I told his wife Patricia and him that the vote would be decided by a handful or fewer ballots. It was like I possessed magical information.

As more and more ballots came the day of January 18, I would text him that it was looking more and more promising. I guess it was like feeding exit polls to politicians on Election Day. It's really impossible to explain how much it meant to him being elected on the first ballot. For Pudge, this was about his legacy. For a competitor like him, it was the toughest kind of competition, too, one in which he had no control.

When Catalina Villegas, who works with Pudge, first called me about writing this book, I was beyond excited. After writing for the Dallas Cowboys the last nine years, including two football books, I was more or less a football writer. Which is fine, I love it, but baseball was my first love, my favorite sport growing up. I really enjoyed working with Pudge on this, and it brought back some memories from when I covered the Texas Rangers right out of college in 1997–98.

Catalina was fantastic to work with. I have no idea how she manages everything and Pudge's busy schedule. I'd also like to thank all those who spoke with me for this project, especially John Blake, the communications vice president for the Texas Rangers, who really went above and beyond on this project.

My appreciation for baseball-reference.com, *The Dallas Morning News*, the *Fort Worth Star-Telegram*, the Associated Press, *The Boston Globe*, MLB.com, and *Sports Illustrated*, among others, for valuable research and information in putting this book together.

I'd also like to thank Tom Bast and editor Jeff Fedotin at Triumph Books and my wife, Danielle. I was crankier on deadline than usual with the condensed time, and as usual, she dealt with the brunt of that crankiness.

Much thanks to bilingual genius Roger Fernandez, one of the most talented writers I've ever had the honor of working with, for helping out on multiple fronts.

I really appreciate Nolan Ryan and Jim Leyland giving their time and baseball brilliance with the forewords. And one of the great joys of my life was trading text messages with Jim for a week or so. Yes, Jim Leyland texts.

Finally, there is no way of explaining how much Nate Regan did to help with this book, and he might just be the biggest Texas Rangers fan on the planet. I'm pretty sure he is going to enjoy his first trip to Cooperstown, right around the time this book releases.